# COGNITIVE ADVANTAGE

How Artificial Intelligence is Changing the
Rules for Winning in Business and Government

Richard J. Carter

## ABOUT THE AUTHOR

Richard J. Carter is a computer scientist and strategic advisor to government and industry on emerging technologies and strategic change.

For over 25 years he has applied cutting-edge technologies to solve hard organisational problems. He has worked both as a leader and as a strategic advisor, for start-ups and multinationals, mainly in the IT, telecommunications and defence sectors. He has produced BAFTA-nominated and award-winning video games and has featured in The Guardian, The Times, New Scientist and the BBC.

He currently holds an Honorary research position at the University of Bristol, he is also a Fellow of the Royal Society of Arts, a Fellow of the British Computer Society, and a Chartered IT Professional.

He has a PhD in Complexity Science, a Master's in Business Administration, a Master's in Nanotechnology, a Bachelor's degree in Computer Science and a postgraduate certificate in Law.

# CONTENTS

# ACKNOWLEDGEMENTS

I began working on this book in January 2020. Like everyone else I had to adapt my plans as the coronavirus swept across the globe. But where the global pandemic has disrupted it has also created – new ideas, new relationships and new opportunities. Through the chaos of the last twelve months, I often found refuge in writing this book. I would like to say that sheer perseverance got me over the finishing line but that would do a grave disservice to those who helped me make it happen.

My deepest gratitude goes to Jennifer Manson, my editor and motivator. Covid-19 brought our life trajectories into close orbit as Jennifer's plans had been disrupted which meant that she had the time to help me make this book a reality. I'm still counting my blessings.

My sincerest thanks to my circle of brilliant friends and colleagues: Dean Beale, Oliver Blanthorn, Greg Fisher, Rhett Gayle, Jordan Giddings, Gavin Newson, Simon Pickard, Jason Shepherd, Chris S and Hank Sohota. Your penetrative insights have generated enough thinking material to last me several lifetimes!

My heartfelt thanks to Andrew Piggott for comprehensively reviewing the first draft and demonstrating a grasp of the English language that I aspire to.

Finally, my love to my wife, Sara, and my two children, Henry and Rose. I promise that I won't start writing another book at the same time that a global pandemic breaks out.

# Chapter 1
# Introduction

*'Our technology, our machines, are part of our humanity. We created them to extend ourselves, and that is what is unique about human beings'*[1]

Ray Kurzweil

In 1997 the reigning world champion chess grandmaster, Garry Kasparov, was beaten in a game of chess in just twenty moves by an artificial intelligence (AI) developed by IBM called Deep Blue. Once the inevitable hype and frenzy about machines taking over the world had subsided, what emerged was a more nuanced and powerful vision of the future: Kasparov began to look at how an AI could augment a human player. So-called 'Centaur AI' as it became known – a phrase inspired by the Greek myth of a half-man, half-horse – pitched a human/machine team against other players (human or machine) and other human/machine teams.

This non-traditional way of playing chess is called Freestyle and, in 2005, an online tournament pitched Centaur players (that combined the superlative pattern discovery of an AI with the deep intuition and strategising of a human) against chess playing AI, chess grandmasters and other Centaur teams. The winning team of the tournament (called ZackS) consisted of two amateur human players, Steven Cramton and Stephen Zackery, augmented with three different AI chess engines running on three laptops. They beat a chess grandmaster/AI team.

The secret to their success? They had a sense of which tool at their disposal – one of the three AI chess engines or their own insights – would suggest the best next move to make. By playing to the respective strengths of each member of the team (human and machine) their collective intelligence proved unbeatable.

This story neatly summarises what this book is about: how to make the best use of AI and humans working symbiotically – a collective intelligence – to achieve things that are beyond the capability of either acting alone. This way of thinking about human + machine rather than human vs. machine is beautifully captured in Nicky Case's prize-winning essay in the Journal of Design and Science, '… computers are good at deciding on the best answers; humans are good at deciding on the best questions'[2]. This constructive relationship between human and machine is one that has not received as much attention as we may have expected, and yet it is very likely to be the key to success in chess, in business, in politics and in life.

The relationship between AI and humans is nascent and intrinsically complex and we do not yet know how it may evolve. There are many examples of AI out-competing human intellect: as we have already seen, AI beating world champion chess masters; Deepmind's Alpha Zero AI teaching itself to play Go (which is a far more complex game to learn, let alone master) and to then subsequently beat the world champion. In the medical field the anomaly-detecting prowess of AI has been consistently better at detecting breast cancer from x-rays than human experts.

The quality exhibited by AI that allows it to out-compete humans is the scale and speed of its data processing capacity. This enables many alternative actions to be assessed concurrently based on an analysis of the present situation. Testing vast numbers of alternative hypotheses – primarily in synthetic environments – can yield successful strategies that would simply be too expensive, time-consuming or dangerous for humans experimenting in the real world to discover.

There is a genuine and understandable fear that machines will replace humans in a variety of different work contexts, from the production line to the consultant radiologist. I do not believe it is an exaggeration to suggest that every job that currently exists will be affected – positively and negatively – by AI. We must be cognisant of the effect that our decisions about AI will have on our society, our economy and ourselves.

Even as AI enhances our ability to understand the world around us, and in ways that we cannot yet imagine, we must recognise that with that superhuman capacity to think comes a responsibility for us to see the bigger picture and to act with a greater appreciation of the impact.

We do not yet know whether we will develop a human-valued AI that can determine what is just or fair. We should expect humans to retain primacy over determining whether an action is wise or not. This responsibility for ethical behaviour applies to everyone, whether you are the leader of an advanced nation, a CEO or an engineer. It means that we must be open to changing our minds. It means that we forsake immediate gratification and short-term gains for courses of action where the benefit to us is less obvious, in the hope of cultivating a brighter future for ourselves and the planet.

This is challenging, but as the world around us becomes more digital and metricated (how many steps you have walked today, what food you have eaten, how far you have travelled in your car, etc.) we should have a greater insight into ourselves and our impact in the world. There is, of course, a risk of information overload but that is where AI will help us.

As you read this book, you will discover we need to build a society founded on sagacity. This wonderful term simply means 'wise action from penetrative insight and foresight'[3]. What do we mean by wise? It is a relative term and I use it to mean thoughtful, ethical action that attempts to hold in balance the optimal trade-off between pursuing one's own interests whilst also striving to maximise the 'greater good' for our society and planet. Sagacity is not synonymous with wisdom. Sagacity, as I have intended to use it, is a quality of constantly striving to become wiser.

Sagacity is an activity; the end goal is greater wisdom.

Of course, I am not blind to the fact that we live on a planet with diverse cultures. What is deemed to be ethical, fair action in England may be deemed to be unjust and unfair in Saudi Arabia. And vice versa. Wisdom, and our societal beliefs and norms that drive our evaluation of what is wise or not, is therefore a relative term. When we are using AI to heighten our perception and agency to act, different countries, even different corporations, will have a different bar for what is deemed to be fair and ethical or not.

The law represents the minimum level of moral behaviour in society and will, of course, have a role in determining the threshold for base behaviour when it comes to the use of AI and other cognitive technologies. Law is also relative. So, what is my point? It is simply this: as we adapt to the impact that AI will have on our society, the freedoms to use that technology will vary from country to country. Your rivals and adversaries may not be as hindered by social acceptance in their use of AI as you are.

This presents a profound challenge and will become an increasingly common story. How can you possibly compete when your socio-political homeland – either through law or through voluntary ethical practices – prevent you from embracing the full potential of AI? I do not pretend to have found the answer to this. Instead, I outline how the use of AI could be maximised to develop an advantage when it comes to insight and action.

## Who Should Read This Book?

This book is aimed at innovators, influencers and decision-makers – wherever you may be. The organisations that succeed in the future will be led by those who are comfortable with innovation.

If you are a CEO or CTO or chief data scientist, or otherwise have responsibility for setting the direction of innovation within your organisation, the ideas presented in this book should be of interest. You don't necessarily need a deep technical understanding – just a degree of comfort and interest in reading about technology and human behaviour.

But this book is not aimed only at the C-suite. Indeed, it is not important what role you currently play, because if you're a good innovator, you are likely to be pretty good at influencing other people's ideas. This is how innovations take hold: through people who are willing to explore something new, despite uncertainty in terms of the value of doing so, or of any definable outcome.

If you have accountability for future capabilities; if part of your remit is to turn an avalanche of data into an advantage, then hopefully the ideas in this book will help you achieve your goals.

## A Paradigm Shift

We can see that AI is bringing changes into our world that will define the way human society moves forward. But AI isn't new. The notion of AI is at least 70 years old. The genesis of the modern idea of AI came from Alan Turing in his famous paper, *Computing Machinery and Intelligence*, published in 1950 in *Mind* (which I discuss in Chapter 4). He proposed a way to test whether a general artificial intelligence (that is one that is deemed to be close to, or on a par, with human intelligence) has indeed been created.

Turing's prescient work inspired decades of computer scientists and mathematicians who would eventually invent concepts such as neural networks and genetic algorithms in the late 1980s and early 1990s. However, we had to wait for the start of the new millennium and the rise of the internet, communications technologies and the commoditisation of computer hardware before the potential of these algorithmic models for learning and optimisation could begin to be realised.

The penetration of AI across industry and government is already significant. Investment in AI contributed to a global digital economy that was valued at $11 trillion in 2018, fuelled by the generation of 33 zettabytes of data (the equivalent of 660 billion Blu-ray discs). By 2025, with the expansion of the Internet of Things enabled by adoption of 5G and cloud technologies, the digital economy is forecast to reach a value of $23 trillion – with AI as a major driver of growth – and to be generating nearly 175 zettabytes of data annually.

Within this context, 'data is the new oil'[4] holds some truth as the driver of the digital economy. Insights from data can provide an understanding of what is happening with customers, infrastructure and competitors; but it takes work to extract this value, and simple understanding is not enough. Businesses and governments also need to apply data-driven insight to inform action at sufficient pace to generate precise, high impact effects in their operating environment. AI facilitates augmented and automated decision-making to achieve the speed required.

But we are only just starting out. In 2019 the consulting firm Accenture published a report *AI: Built To Scale* that summarised their findings from interviewing 1,500 C-suite executives from organisations across 16 industries on how much AI was enabling their business strategy now and in the future. In total 84% of executives believed that they would not achieve their business objectives unless they scaled up their use of AI; yet 76% acknowledged that they do not know how to do this; and 75% believed that they risked going out of business *within 5 years* if they did not successfully scale AI.

In the same way that it would be unthinkable now to run an organisation without computers – whereas 20 years ago that would still have been possible – in another decade it will be unthinkable for an organisation to function without a fleet of AI capabilities that enhances human capabilities.

## Moving from Information Advantage to Cognitive Advantage

As soon as computers and the internet really started to have an impact in the world people started talking about information advantage. Big Data is one of the drivers of information advantage. The idea is that if you can sift through vast swathes of noise to pick out certain bits of information that inform your understanding of the environment, that will give you an advantage, a better understanding of the environment than your competitors or adversaries.

However, information advantage doesn't convey action and so it doesn't capture an AI world. Action as a response to understanding is essential. In the new world we have moved into, AI is about automated decision-making in a continual cycle of comprehending and acting.

As AI takes us from the existing paradigm – of seeking an information advantage as the basis of competing successfully – to one of hyper-accelerated decision-making, how do we compete in a world where everyone is investing in AI to make better and quicker decisions?

In other words, as we reach the limit of what AI can do for us (in the mathematical definition of the word 'limit' where further changes are infinitesimally small) and as we saturate our use of AI such that all competitive players are taking advantage of it, how do we succeed?

I advocate that the main driver for success in this new paradigm is the ability to shape the environment that is generating the world's data – the information domain. The focus therefore needs to be on building and maintaining operational capabilities that enable deep, insightful action in this domain.

This yields a cognitive advantage which I define as:

*The demonstrable superiority gained through comprehending and acting to shape a competitive environment at a pace and with an ingenuity that an adversary's ability to comprehend and act is compromised*

Consequently, the rival that has an insufficient understanding of their environment will make poor decisions that are little better than random chance. As time goes by, and without drastic intervention, this will lead to further regression of their ability to act with impact.

Cognitive advantage is about understanding the operating environment to enable rapid exploration of options, to then take precise and deliberate action to successfully shape the environment in the organisation's favour; and to do so at pace. Cognitive advantage builds on the concept of information advantage by explicitly including elements of decision-making, such as comprehension, prediction, goal setting, evaluation of alternatives and action. It is an approach that requires the effective fusion of artificial and human intellects.

The additional element of cognitive advantage – recognising that our actions are as important as our ability to understand the environment – is vital in an AI world, where action can be happening at a speed and a scale that is incomprehensible to humans. The ability to act at a massive scale with confidence requires deep insights, not just into what is happening in the environment, but also deep insight and foresight into the likely impact of our actions and that of our AI in that environment.

A cognitive advantage will be the new basis for power in an AI-rich world. Yet there is a duality to holding a cognitive advantage: the power to compete and win can also be used to cultivate a sustainable operating environment for the organisation.

This latter point can be described as acting with sagacity, and can sometimes lead to action that appears counterintuitive, for example, where an organisation is both competing against but also cooperating with another organisation (such as Apple and Samsung who compete in the smartphone market whilst also cooperating to supply Samsung display technologies for use in Apple products).

I'll now describe these two aspects of cognitive advantage.

## Outpacing and Out-Innovating Adversaries

An important aspect of outpacing adversaries is controlling information flow, influencing what people believe about the world, and therefore how they are likely to act. In terms of building a cognitive advantage, it is not enough to think about strategies and tactics to win. It is about having the right levers and the right resources to have the highest impact within the environment – the ability to act to change people's opinions in the real world.

In recent times, an illuminating example of this is the Leave Campaign's strategy during the UK EU referendum. They used data scientists and mathematicians to look at vast amounts of data, about what people were saying and who those people were connected to on big social networks like Facebook. Using sentiment analysis, and other information that Facebook provides for a fee, they were able to understand the general mood, what people were saying, and what they seemed to care about – and what they liked and didn't like. This data analysis allowed the Leave Team to pin down, with surgical precision, certain voters whom they felt could be persuaded to vote in favour of the Leave Campaign, with a little bit of a nudge.

The Leave Campaign's ability to comprehend a very complex space – the whole spectrum of narratives that were in the British population around the time of the EU Referendum – gave them deep insights into where they could begin to act. They used hundreds, perhaps thousands, of different Facebook ads targeted at the various subsections of the social network they were interested in – the people who could potentially be nudged. There were all sorts of different ways in which these messages could land, so they tried lots of subtly different messages on Facebook; and analysed the data at the same time, creating a feedback loop where they could comprehend, act, and then comprehend the effect of their actions. Through that process they were continually iterating and narrowing in on the messaging that seemed to be having the greatest effect.

Compare that to the Remain Campaign, which relied mainly on traditional modes of reaching the population, such as getting celebrities to endorse staying in the EU and traveling around the UK on buses. Yes, the Leave Campaign did that as well, but the Remain Campaign did not appear to take the data-rich approach to strategy; and the fact that there was a surprising result could well indicate that the Leave Campaign's approach gave it an advantage.

Amazon Web Services (AWS) is another interesting example of out-pacing adversaries. Cloud computing didn't exist as a market sector 18 years ago and yet it has expanded rapidly to now be valued at $832 billion by 2025. It is a highly competitive market. Selective pressures in this market are the reliability and the diversity of services/capabilities that are available on cloud platforms. AWS have clearly understood this and have spent well over a decade cultivating a workforce that is relentlessly focused on constant innovation, constant disruption, and a constant need to change. They use machine learning to understand what kind of services people are using and then they quickly adapt their own offering to follow where they see trends occurring. This isn't happening in days or weeks or months. This is happening within hours. In 2019, Amazon boasted that they were releasing over 2000 new software capabilities every day.

Let's think about that for a moment. Clearly humans are not the only actors in making that happen. It is inconceivable that a human, or a team of humans, could analyse the environment, understand where people are using software in a different way, and create/test/deploy 2000 capabilities daily. There is likely to be a significant use of automated and augmented decision-making enabling such scale and pace.

There are two aspects of interest here: one is the superior effectiveness of their data analysis; the other is the fact that the pace and the diversity and the scale of what they are bringing into the marketplace is completely disrupting the environment for their competition. That scale and scope and pace give them an unassailable leader advantage. How they are using data and machine learning on their own platform enables that.

Controlling information flow isn't just about voters and consumers; it also relates to how your rival perceives their world. And their perception of their environment and their situation will determine what action they take. If they have a faulty perception of the environment – either because they can't comprehend the environment through a lack of data, or poor quality data, or a lack of analytical skills, or because someone is deliberately misleading them, or because the environment is changing too fast to keep up – their subsequent decisions will be low quality, and their actions ineffective.

Having a cognitive advantage means keeping ahead of the competition in a way that impacts their ability to comprehend and therefore act effectively. The faster we go through that perception-action cycle, the more we can compromise our adversary's power to do so, because the environment is changing in a way that is too complex for them to comprehend, or simply too fast for them to keep up. It becomes increasingly difficult for humans to compete on that accelerated perception-action loop without using AI.

In 2017, the US Air Force's General Goldfein succinctly captured the transformation underway in defence and national security when he stated that '... we're transitioning from wars of attrition to wars of cognition...'[5]. Taken to its logical conclusion, cognitive advantage leads to an adversary experiencing cognitive fatigue, which renders them incapable of keeping up with, or effectively responding to, their environment. Of course, the exit of an adversary from an environment may have its own consequences; the organisation holding a cognitive advantage would have foreseen the effect of such an event.

## Acting Sagaciously

The examples of the Leave Campaign and Amazon starkly illustrate how data insight and the ability to act at speed can lead to outcompeting competitors. But it is not, as I see it, a true example of cognitive advantage, because cognitive advantage has a deeper, wiser, more long-term strategic aspect. Cognitive advantage is about sagacity.

Sagacity means acting with acute insight and wisdom. Acting sagaciously is thinking and acting in the best interests of the long-term viability of the ecosystem in which an organisation exists. I don't see sagacity as being purely about altruism (although that may play a part); I see it as the holistic view of the role and impact an organisation has in its environment, and its interdependency with its environment.

When we think beyond the next quarterly report to shareholders, perhaps 10 or 20 years into the future to the long-term impact, then shaping the environment links our success to the success of our ecosystem. This is a wiser, more mature view of shaping the environment for our own advantage.

Every person, team, company or government has the possibility of bringing wisdom – sagacity – to its operation. Collectively, an organisation can make astute assessments of what is going on and form wise and humane views on what it should do next, to have the most beneficial impact in its ecosystem.

Ecosystems (whether political, business, social) are continually disrupted because players are constantly innovating and constantly striving to outcompete and outmanoeuvre other players. This is also true for social, political and commercial ecosystems. We need to understand the environment of our ecosystem, and to be able to predict how it is likely to change. That gives us the ability to plan, and beyond that, the ability to shape the environment to the advantage of the organisation, the people we serve and to the long-term viability of the ecosystem on which we depend.

Governments create an ecosystem that allow others to succeed, and in the same way, companies can cultivate their own ecosystems to create market opportunities for themselves and their partners. For technology platforms, such as Facebook, YouTube, and so on, it is in their interests to act for the good of the customers who participate on their platforms (with some finding this easier to do than others).

In this scenario our society is lifted. I don't want to call it an 'enlightenment' because that language carries preconceptions with it, but it opens the way to more sophisticated, responsible behaviour than we have exhibited throughout history. Sagacity as a concept is helpful, because it conveys the idea that with power comes responsibility. To succeed in this more advanced society will require foresight. We will need to be able to make sense of our environment, understand and accurately translate and interpret what is happening in that environment, and take the most effective action, in the shortest timescale, for the maximum benefit not just to our own organisation, but to the rest of the ecosystem in which we exist. Where action may not be appropriate, we at least need to be prepared for a possible outcome.

On a global level, China's sometimes surprising actions in the wider world may hint at sagacious thinking. As part of their Belt and Road initiative, China is investing billions into infrastructure projects around the world; and doing so with few apparent strings attached. They are playing a long game, and it seems it may be a very smart move. Infrastructure shapes environment. It dictates the movement of people and of goods. As a country, they appear to be pursuing a cognitive advantage trajectory and are positioning themselves to shape the world in unforeseeable ways. This global expansion is generating consequences such as de-forestation and $CO_2$ emissions; and humanitarian concerns will remain a significant challenge.

The level of sagacity they bring to this endeavour remains to be seen.

## Data, Data Everywhere but Not a Byte to Eat

This is a riff on the saying from the Rime of the Ancient Mariner. He had survived a shipwreck, and he was on a raft, dying of thirst. He said, 'Water, water everywhere, and not a drop to drink'[6]. The new world of data feels a bit like that. We are awash with data but a lot of it is noise; some of it is toxic, so you want to avoid that; some of it is fake, so it's going to mislead you and waste your time. You'll expend cognitive effort on fabricated data. The data you are interested in is probably a very tiny fraction of the data that might be available to you.

Every organisation has an informational limit: the amount of data it can gather and process to inform action. There is a finite limit to the physical resources (people, money) and the technical resources (data analysis capabilities, knowledge) available to make use of data and so the challenge is in optimising the data aperture of the organisation. This is an iterative process, requiring capabilities in data analysis, in understanding how, why and where data is generated, and interpreting the value of the data in terms of impact. Some investment is required to start the process, with initial trial and error followed by continuous learning to inform and refine what data is needed.

The needs of customers/citizens are changing on a daily, even hourly, basis. Real-time, continuous feedback of large amounts of data from which to identify patterns and emerging trends to comprehend what is happening and what may happen next, is the hallmark of a digitally capable organisation. We only need to look at the empty supermarket shelves that appeared in

March 2020, as the Covid-19 pandemic began, to see the consequences of failing to spot these patterns, or a lack of data, or failing to maintain sufficient resilience to respond to potential change.

## Collective Intelligence

Let's come back now to the concept I introduced earlier, of collective intelligence, to understand what I mean by it in the context of data. Individuals perceive and comprehend things differently from each other; in groups, comprehension changes and knowledge is created through a dialectic process, with people informing and being informed by each other's opinions.

For much of the second half of the 20th century, most organisations cultivated a 'hero culture', with everyone looking at the leader as an all-knowing mind. In the new, fast-moving world of automated systems, this isn't going to work anymore. It neglects the power and value of the information that is held throughout the organisation. Google, for example, takes a more distributed approach to leadership. The founders recognised that for Google to really flourish and grow, they needed to cultivate a culture where everyone was encouraged to openly innovate and to lead in their own unique way.

As information and knowledge pass between individuals and teams, up to the more ephemeral organisational level, there is dialectic influence here as well. The integration of these information feeds gives rise to a mutual understanding of the current state of the operating environment. Collective intelligence arises from reasoning about shared information.

That collective intelligence is greater than the sum of the parts – there is emergence, in the complexity science sense. From that collective intelligence emerges understanding, realisation and insight that no individual in that organisation could have reached alone. Organisational understanding, or corporate understanding, comes from the collective understanding of all elements.

## Using our 50 Bits Per Second Wisely

It is estimated that when we are reading a book or solving a puzzle, our conscious mind processes a maximum of just 50 bits a second. This is a very slow, very expensive (albeit powerful) cognitive load, so it is important to optimise the use of this precious resource. For reference, the Nvidia GTX 960, a cheap consumer graphics card from 2015, has a throughput of about 50 gigabits per second: a billion times more.

The functions of cognition – sensory input, encoding, processing, meaning – can be viewed as a hierarchy: data at the bottom, then information, knowledge and finally wisdom at the top, the scarcest and most valuable. Nowadays, many humans are using their 50 bps down at the data level. In an AI world, that no longer needs to be the case. Ideally the genius of our über-expensive but talented, compassionate and moralistic humans should be focused on wisdom, where we can add the most value, and let AI do as much as possible of the rest.

The huge amount of information and knowledge needs to be encoded in a form that is accessible to both artificial and human intellect alike. Data-linked models deployed across computing infrastructure and digital devices will provide the flexibility and the scalability required. This is an encoding of the unified understanding that the collective intelligence of an organisation has on the environment, as well as the means to query, explore and update it. Cognitive functions such as reasoning, learning and knowledge retrieval provide access into this knowledge store.

The human-machine interface must be high priority if we are to extract the maximum value from the collective intelligence of our artificial and human intellects. We can learn from the videogames industry here; they are, after all, experts in creating large-scale virtual worlds that equip humans – often with AI working alongside them – with the ability to act and to problem solve to win in a rapidly changing simulated world, competing against other artificial and human players.

## The Cognitive Enterprise

I advocate that we consciously design our organisations to maximise the collective intelligence of human and artificial workforces as a critical, protected asset. The interdependency and interflow of ideas, knowledge and information between all human and artificial entities is what gives the edge to the organisation having a cognitive advantage. I call this type of organisation a cognitive enterprise.

A cognitive enterprise prioritises deeply insightful and far-sighted action to shape an operating environment as the means for success. The cognitive enterprise, as I am suggesting we design it, encodes these insights into the architecture of the organisation: the design of processes; the types of people and skills employed; the software; the hardware. The architecture of the enterprise is centred on cognitive functions that optimise the informational and operational limits of the organisation.

The critical centre of the cognitive enterprise is something I call a 'synthetic core' – an encoded representation of everything that the organisation has learned and continues to learn about itself and its environment. This body of knowledge and meaning becomes an organisation's most prized asset. It forms a critical part of all cognitive processes, and is queried, explored and updated by the collective intelligence of the organisation. An effective synthetic core requires the integration of a diverse range of capabilities in artificial intelligence, behavioural science, cloud computing, complexity science, data science, decision science, knowledge management and simulation environments.

Embracing technological developments such as augmented and virtual reality, haptics, data visualisation, simulations and natural language processing will enable humans to fully utilise the synthetic core.

The cognitive enterprise will yield a powerful capability to be used responsibly. We will need to build a culture that values sustainment and cultivation more than disruption and exploitation. We may find that AI, by helping us gain a deeper insight into the options available to us and the likely consequences of our actions, enables us to adopt such values. Having a cognitive advantage will help us on that journey.

## Summary

Cognitive advantage is about:

- Sensing, thinking and moving faster than your rivals and adversaries, and maximising the use of AI to do this

- Being sufficiently self-aware of the fit of the organisation to the operating environment; continually adapting to optimise the collective intelligence of the organisation

- Relentlessly shaping the operating environment to maintain a cognitive advantage whilst simultaneously cultivating its long-term viability

Keeping up and staying ahead is not only about responding and adapting to changes in the operating environment. Ultimately, it is about shaping the operating environment, enabled through having a cognitive advantage. Understanding this introduces a shift in how we think about the ideal organisation. Whilst agile organisations are currently seen as the exemplar for being successful, in an AI rich 'cognitive' world, being responsive to change is not enough.

Agile organisations respond, sagacious organisations shape.

To become a sagacious organisation requires foresight and a willingness to act, even when there is no immediate threat to the organisation. It is about asking:

'If we were starting from a blank canvas and we knew about the AI capability that is coming, how would we organise ourselves to best take advantage of this? How would we organise ourselves to make the most of what's now possible, so that we can launch ourselves onto a cognitive advantage trajectory? And how can we do all that in such a way that we shape the environment we operate in so that it thrives?'[7]

These are the questions I have been asked to think about, and that have arisen, over the past decade, as I have worked with organisations facing a powerful need to change. This book shares some of what I have discovered in that time; I also sketch out some ideas on how we think about the fusion of humans + AI and what I believe may (or should) happen as society embraces AI. I consider what capabilities we may need to build, how we may need to organise ourselves and how we should think anew about leadership. Implicit throughout is my belief that we should set new expectations for ourselves and each other to act with sagacity.

Chapter 2 considers the big picture. What are the major technological, sociocultural and geopolitical trends that are driving changes in our world? If we are seeking to become an organisation that shapes rather than simply responds to changes then we will need to cultivate a deep understanding of the complex environment that we are operating in. Developing a cognitive advantage will help us do this.

Chapter 3 introduces you to a concept called autopoiesis which means self-producing or self-maintaining. It is a simple yet powerful idea for understanding why some forms of organisation (a biological cell, an organism, a human, an entire civilisation) can endure over time. Adaptation is a key attribute of such systems and that emerges from two processes – autonomy and cognition – which I also describe.

Chapter 4 explore ideas for how we may apply AI to help humans make better decisions. In particular, I introduce Judea Pearl's work on causality which I adopt as a useful framework to think about human + AI reasoning and collaboration. This chapter is not an exhaustive examination of AI although I do summarise the main topics of the field.

Chapter 5 considers the role that complexity science has in helping us to attain a cognitive advantage. We will need to build a shared causal understanding of a world that is of interest to us. We will need to go upstream of the data we collect and seek to understand the real-world system (and virtual worlds too) that has generated the data. Many real-world processes are non-linear, and in that case, predicting an outcome from the occurrence of an event is generally poor, due to small variations in the conditions that caused the event leading to large changes in the effect. This makes inferring causality very challenging. Complexity science will be a critical tool in helping us to make progress here. Pearl's work on causality makes another appearance here too.

Chapter 6 focuses on leadership. What are successful future leaders going to look like in an AI-rich, hyper-accelerated world? What will they need to be good at? I have already suggested that our leaders need to exhibit the quality of sagacity: acting on penetrative insight to make decisions that are competitive and that cultivate the long-term sustainability of their organisation's operating environment. The tension in achieving both is inherent to the leadership challenge that is coming. AI can help, but it may also hinder. We need to start thinking now about the type of leaders we need and the type of culture that we foster such that we inspire and elicit the best from the collective intelligence of our enterprise.

Chapter 7 looks at how we influence the behaviours of others and, subsequently, shape the environment that we operate in. I make the distinction between two domains in which we (and AI) can operate: the physical domain and the information domain. I also touch on topics related to sourcing and using data to inform action; and briefly introduce you to ideas for doing so ethically.

Chapter 8 is where we begin bringing it all together as I expand on the idea of the cognitive enterprise: getting the right data, to the right intellect, at the right time, to have the right impact, guided by the right values. The goal of the cognitive enterprise is to do this efficiently, seamlessly and continuously. I describe what the cognitive enterprise is and suggest some design principles for how to build one e.g., the idea of a 'cognitive agent' as the focal point for the designers, engineers and architects who will build the cognitive enterprise.

Chapter 9 describes six goals to be pursued in building and maintaining a cognitive advantage. The challenges that may lie ahead are significant. Some will be self-fulfilling – such as gaining an impetus to change, re-skilling your workforce, making good investments, beginning the complex task of shifting your organisation's culture. Some will be external and to do with competing for scarce resources and understanding the journey you need to take your customers or citizens on. My recommendation is to bootstrap; begin by building a minimal version of a cognitive enterprise that will enable you to achieve an objective that you would not otherwise have been able to pursue.

Whenever there is a paradigm shift in technology – the integrated circuit, the internet, mobile communication technology – there are those organisations that fail to adapt. The new paradigm of hyper-accelerated decision-making enabled by AI is no different. I hope that this book helps you to do more than adapt. I hope that it helps you to shape and to thrive in our increasingly complex and uncertain world.

# Chapter 2
# Forces of Change

*'The world is changing faster than we can learn about it.'*[8]

Eddie Obeng

In this chapter I want to highlight some of the major forces of change that are already shaping our world and that will continue to do so over the next 10 – 20 years. My intent is twofold: firstly, resistance to these changes is futile and so being forewarned allows a degree of time and space to be prepared if you are not already; and secondly, this is the world that we all operate in individually (as citizens) and collectively (as part of a company or government) and we need to understand that our actions can shape this environment.

We are responding to our environment almost all the time (when we are not simply overwhelmed by it), and yet we need to get ahead of the curve and be the agents changing that environment. We want to encourage our customers and our adversaries to choose options from this shared environment because that choice confers a benefit to us. We need to understand this environment sufficiently well to devise strategies and tactics that give us the best *bang per buck* for where we place our bets and where we make our moves.

## A Web of Wicked Problems

I think we can all relate to Eddie Obeng's quotation at the beginning of this chapter: the insatiable drive of new technology, surprising outcomes in politics, the creative destruction in our social norms as we become a global, hyper-connected community, nature once again showing us who is boss with global pandemics and climate change.

The rate at which change is happening only seems to be accelerating and these increasingly turbulent times bring with them increased uncertainty over what to make of it all and what to do. We are living in a world where evidence of the *Law of Unintended Consequences* is all around us. For example, that new bypass road that is put in at significant cost to reduce congestion, only to itself get congested within a few years, thus just shifting the problem to a different road; or a government increasing taxation to help pay for public services and inadvertently reducing demand for goods and services, thus causing a recession which reduces tax revenues below what they were before the increase in taxation. And so on.

We are surrounded by *wicked problems* a term coined by Horst Rittel & Melvin Webber (in their 1973 treatise *Dilemmas in a General Theory of Planning*) to mean an entangled web of cause and effect where it is extremely difficult, if not impossible, to identify the origin or the ordering of a cause-and-effect relationship. This means that as humans, and for any systems that we may seek to design and engineer, it is increasingly hard to ensure we have the effect we intend.

Tackling a wicked problem yields a 'bit better' or 'less bad' outcome, rather than the simple right or wrong answer we think we are going to get. In other words, we need to get comfortable with being uncomfortable about the effects of our actions; we need to accept that the only certainty now is uncertainty.

This world – that is changing faster than we can learn about it – is a rapidly growing and increasingly diverse web of wicked problems, meaning that our ability to predict possible future outcomes is correspondingly uncertain. In response to that, both individually and as organisations, we need to embrace that uncertainty and to see it as a challenge.

AI is a critical tool to help us to get good at dealing with uncertainty and for investigating wicked problems. If we design AI into our sense-making and decision-making systems in the right way, we could deploy AI to explore, experiment and investigate hundreds, thousands, possibly even millions of alternative possible courses of action – testing out hypotheses about possible future outcomes – at a pace that we as humans alone could not even remotely achieve unaided.

## A Warming World

In their 2014 report, the International Panel on Climate Change stated that: 'Human influence on the climate system is clear.... [and] recent climate changes have had widespread impacts on human and natural systems'[9]. Our atmosphere and our oceans are getting warmer, snow and ice are reducing around the world, and there is a continued rise in sea levels. These changes are based on objective, quantifiable and verifiable data that has been meticulously collected and rigorously analysed.

The association here is clear: a warmer climate leads to the melting of snow and ice which ends up in our rivers and oceans. And, to demonstrate the wickedness of this problem: as our atmosphere warms up, more snow and ice melts, meaning less sunlight is reflected into the atmosphere, thus warming up our oceans in a positive feedback loop (which will be discussed further in Chapter 5).

The cause of climate change is anthropogenic greenhouse gas emissions. In other words, us. We are the cause. Or, at least, it is extremely likely that we are the cause: our industries, our modern society, our lifestyle. Our economic system is reliant on the production and the transport of goods. The internet is dependent on energy which still comes largely from the burning of fossil fuels.

Climate change requires global cooperation and yet we do not have a coherent global system of governance. The United Nations can only intervene to a degree, and the International Panel on Climate Change can only advise. Addressing climate change is the responsibility of every government and their citizens. It is a truly wicked problem, and we must act, whether that is as private citizens voting with their wallets, as employees demanding more from corporate social responsibility, or as elected politicians and leaders who realise that tangible and transparent action is the only way to tackle this issue.

As a global society, we need to do something about climate change – that is a given. Fortunately, the deep insights that AI and data science can give us are not only available to serve the incumbent powers: they are also available to those subsections of society who will hold organisations and governments to account.

Using AI and data science to generate evidence independently of formal institutions will become an increasingly powerful tool for organised citizen groups to fact-check official figures and reports. This forms a trusted alternative source of information which acts as a counterbalance to officially sanctioned information. This should generate more for official organisations to demonstrably act in the interests of the people they nominally serve. If that is accepted as a plausible scenario, a foresighted politician or chief executive needs to be thinking about transparency.

In the past, dubious actions could be swept under the carpet, decisions could be made in the service of making quarterly earnings look good, and the PR department could take care of the rest. Those days are fading, and accountability for past decisions may come back to bite. It is a burning platform for chief execs and politicians.

## A Growing and Aging Population

Adding to this is the fact that, as of August 2020, the total population on planet earth was estimated at 7.6 billion people and is forecast to grow to 11.2 billion people by 2099. Most of that population growth is estimated to occur in Asia and Africa – two continents that are not geared towards the reduction of greenhouse gas emissions.

The demographics of our population are changing. People are living longer, which means their experience and skills should continue to benefit society and the economy. The expectation for most of a population to retire on a good pension at 65 is unlikely to exist in 10 or 20 years from now (indeed I suspect we are already approaching this point). Rather, the norm will be to continue to contribute to society in mind, body and spirit, rather than taking a step back. This means we will have very skilled and experienced knowledge workers who are still an important part of our economy and society.

We don't yet know what the impact of that split will be, between the older, perhaps wiser, perhaps more sagacious individuals in the aging population, and the younger, highly adaptable, risk-taking population. There are all sorts of implications of an aging population in a cognitive advantage world; embracing the aging population for the benefit of making wiser, more sagacious decisions may be very important. It is time to reassess the value of people who, traditionally, we would have perceived as being ready to retire.

Of course, sagacity is not exclusive to those of advanced years – anyone of any age can be sagacious – but there is far more that we can do in our institutions to inform wise action from blending the beliefs and experiences of people across the full spectrum of age groups.

## Information Overload

We are living in an unprecedented time of change where we are constantly bombarded with new information. Every hour of every day it can feel like we are being told to do this, stop eating that, don't do that, boycott that person, and so on. We are constantly hit with conflicting views and it is incredibly difficult to make sense of it all. We are now connected far more than we have ever been, and this has created a true dichotomy: good news, we are hyper-connected; bad news, we are hyper-connected.

Fewer of us feel as though we are coping. We don't know which way is up and this can leave us feeling helpless. Any action we may take to modify our own lifestyles – buying an electric car, for example – can feel futile as we observe our neighbour buying a brand new 6.0L V12 pick-up truck. Or we hear climate change deniers telling us that it's all a lie promulgated by left-wing activists. So, although climate change has been empirically shown to be a real thing, we can feel quite helpless.

In times past, information was either oral or it was written down in a book, and information was available, but it wasn't pushed to us, it wasn't forced into our faces 24/7; but that is now the world that we live in. Our ability to sift the nuggets of valuable information – that will help us in our lives and help us do what we want to do – from the overwhelming sea of noise is becoming increasingly overstretched. Ironically, technology will also help solve that problem, reducing that noise floor through AI and machine learning, working out what is and isn't relevant for us. We already see this in recommendation systems – Netflix, Amazon, Google search. Things pop up that are spookily relevant to us. And sometimes they fail.

The Big Data metrics are relevant here: Volume, Velocity, Variety, Veracity. Big Data was recognised as a major influence 10-15 years ago and we are going to have to continue to explore how to manage and make use of an exponential growth in data. There are some major technological drivers, including 5G, and the internet-of-things. 5G will be a hundred times faster than 4G, with lower latency.

That translates into having smart devices embedded into everything around us, communicating with us, with our smartphones, with each other, and with sophisticated algorithms running in the cloud – much faster, and with much lower risks of failure than we have ever seen before. We have new, super-fast fibre technology and are moving into a world of artificial cyber-infrastructure, where humans generate an extremely small fraction of the data that is transmitted over our data networks. Most of the data will be AI and machines talking either to humans or other machines.

We don't yet fully understand what that means for us, as humans. This is why it is so important for us to lower the noise floor, as individuals, as organisations, as governments, so that we are able to get to the data that is important to us. We need to be able to sort for the data that is valuable and relevant, and to process that data to derive appropriate meaning, so that we can make the best decisions possible. The efficacy with which we make decisions relies on being intelligent about the data we spend our time and resources analysing, and how we then use that to inform our actions.

Cognitive fatigue occurs when we reach a point where we are incapable of functioning cognitively – a common experience in this fast-changing world. One significant result is that we fail to comprehend what is going on – because it is too complex or changing too quickly – and because we fail to comprehend, we either don't act, or we act wrongly. As Daniel Kahneman describes it, the *fast-thinking* side of our brain tends to take over when the *slow-thinking* side can't cope.

We carry around with us a certain level of information in our heads. As with a computer, we have a certain amount of working memory, and if we start to run out of memory, that slows down the ability to compute, to complete the task. Our cognitive load is how much we have to think about at any one time. As individuals, as an organisation, or as a society, we carry a cognitive load, and the more uncertain our circumstances, the more our environment is changing, the more turbulence there is in the environment, the higher the cognitive load, because we are trying to understand the environment. That extra work is stressful.

With Covid-19, many people are either struggling to sleep, or feel exhausted all the time. It is not that we are doing anything physical, it is the fact that our brains are working overtime just trying to make sense of what is going on in the world.

Cognitive load doesn't signify quality, it is simply a measure of quantity. We then need to distinguish when the level of cognitive load is leading to cognitive fatigue. Cognitive fatigue is a measure of quality. It is a description of a certain state, where we are no longer able to process information in the environment effectively.

According to the management consultancy firm McKinsey a certain amount of stress is good and necessary. Too little stress or too much stress negatively impact performance. There is an optimal state, and it helps if we are attuned, so that we notice when we start to go to the wrong side of the curve – either through technology that prompts us, or general self-awareness. It is important to know when we are not making progress – when to put down our tools. Some people never learn this and carry on, progressively under-performing, stressed out, working longer and longer hours, because that is the only option they can see.

For many reasons it is important that organisations invest in understanding, at any moment in time, the current level of fatigue of their organisation and the people who work within it. Once again, this isn't being altruistic, it is understanding that our ability to comprehend and act in our environment is a function of the level of cognitive load of the organisation. It is in the leaders' interests to have happy, healthy people who are working close to their peak performance.

This goes further when the information coming in is inaccurate. False data is a poison for people and organisations, consuming perception-action-loop cycles, distracting, leading to poor hypotheses, false conclusions and poor decisions. It is 'kryptonite' for an organisation that is pursuing a cognitive advantage trajectory. Knowing the optimum level of investment in confirming the veracity of the organisation's data is vitally important.

Data from a trusted source will cost, but trusted, high-value, proprietary data is like gold; that data will be being automatically fed into the semantic graph of the organisation, and the whole AI capability stack will be using that semantic graph to operate on.

If the semantic graph is inaccurate because it has been populated with false data, AI will make weird, unhelpful and costly decisions on the organisation's behalf. It is important to understand the impact fake data would have on a truly data-driven organisation, and to ensure that the provenance and veracity of data sources can be verified.

Our ability to comprehend how the world is changing with our 50 bits/s of conscious analysis – very powerful, but very slow, very expensive – we just can't comprehend everything. I think we all have a sense from time to time of being utterly overwhelmed by the information around us, getting drawn into subjects that for whatever reason have attracted our attention, but that have no real value to us. We are surrounded by constant noise and occasionally some snippets of information rise above the noise floor and get our attention, but they are not necessarily the most valuable things, or the things that are going to help us.

It is interesting to note that the AI that, as individuals, we are most familiar with – Amazon Alexa, Google Search, Netflix – is geared towards helping us to consume more. We are sleepwalking into a situation where our use of AI is restricting us to being consumers, rather than elevating our ability to achieve our goals in life. If we are to cut through the wicked problems in our private and professional lives, then we need to start to think about how AI augments us as beautifully illustrated by 'Centaur' chess teams.

When our cognitive load is too great, the instinctive behaviours of fight, flight or freeze can take over. We can no longer comprehend what is going on, and our options are to run away, freeze in place, or attack, even though we don't really comprehend what we are attacking. Cognitive fatigue is a very bad situation for individuals; and there is also an organisational version: Kodak is an example of a company that demonstrated cognitive fatigue. Unable to comprehend the impact of digital technology in its environment, primarily because the environment was changing in ways and at a speed that Kodak could not make sense of it and, because of that, they were unable or unwilling to change their business model.

Cognitive advantage is a way of addressing cognitive fatigue – giving us a strategy by which we can comprehend the environment and generate appropriate action. We need to get good at this, otherwise we are not going to survive; and we can also use this knowledge in our favour, and work to change our competitors' environment beyond their ability to comprehend. Cognitive fatigue in our competitors means advantage for ourselves. This will become the essential element in competition: maintaining cognitive ability when the environment is changing at an ever-increasing rate. Wicked problems will make up the landscape of the future.

## Changing Cultural Values and Expectations

In Western society (and as most visibly demonstrated by Generation Z who are those people born between 1997 and 2012 and whom Greta Thunberg is an exemplar) we are becoming less driven by money, job security and status. Instead, we are beginning to cultivate a deeper understanding of ourselves and our role in society. Even though recent years may have had a vibrant tone of self-promotion about them – as evidenced by the popularity of TikTok, Instagram and the pseudo-celebrity culture – there may be signs we are moving on from that. Authenticity is now emerging as a more valued trait. This is important to any human being, to feel a sense of authenticity, but it seems to be even more important in a cyber world where it is easy to fabricate in order to fit in or to stand out.

A rejection of faking it on social media is giving way to favouring and demonstrating an allegiance to things that are more meaningful. Again, to use Generation Z as the primary movers here, we are now more likely to boycott products and less likely to take jobs with multinational corporations who can't demonstrate a commitment to socially acceptable behaviour and responsible action to the environment. I do recognise that, in some cases, such actions are driven by cynical rather than genuine altruistic motives but, on the whole, I believe that we are becoming a more considerate society. Our shared shock and grief throughout the Covid-19 pandemic has revealed the similarities, rather than the differences, between us and this fuels our compassion.

People, Planet and Profit is a notion that has been talked about since the '80s – sometimes authentically, sometimes cynically. With these upcoming generations, that Triple-Bottom-Line thinking will become more mainstream, massively enabled by emerging technology. Policy, with respect to the environment, will need to change.

Public perception of organisations and governments is based on what they are seen to be doing to help climate change, or not. Some of that is very visible, overt, as was the case with Donald Trump; but a lot of the time, where it really matters is behind closed doors, with people working to turn policy into legislation. Big Data, machine learning and AI are going to make it difficult to hide that. For tech-savvy digital natives, finding out what a policy maker is doing will be like going for a walk down the street to look over a garden wall.

There will be fewer places for governments and big corporations to hide – so rather than just paying lip-service to acting responsibly in creating and contributing to a fairer and more sustainable society, organisations will need to be transparent, and put real, empirical evidence on the table, as to what they are doing or not doing. We have lacked the means to quantify the People and Planet aspects of the eventual bottom line. With AI and data, that will no longer be the case.

The #MeToo movement is exposing things that happened up to 40 or 50 years ago, and perpetrators of those times are being held to the standards of these. Wise leaders will act today in anticipation of future transparency, and the likelihood of being held accountable to future standards of behaviour. Foresight requires thinking through what those standards are likely to be. The fact that something has not previously been called out, and no one has ever held up the mirror, doesn't mean society won't expect us to have been guided by higher levels of self-judgement. The imperative of maximising shareholder value will not excuse lapses in broader societal and environmental accountability. There are now fewer places to hide unethical practices.

Von Hippel's book *The Democratisation of Innovation* describes the phenomenon of new products being crowd-sourced, rather than being put together by a team of specialist designers, for example, software products such as the Linux operating system or the Firefox browser. This is a phenomenon observed in the early years of the internet and was driven by the ability for geographically dispersed but like-minded individuals to share knowledge, skills and purpose. In the second decade of the 21$^{st}$ century, we see crowdsourcing of analytical effort to perform citizen-led investigations that would traditionally have been the preserve of intelligence agencies or professional journalists.

A high-profile example of this is Bellingcat which demonstrates the ability of a group of volunteers to coordinate their skills, knowledge and time to pursue investigations in a self-organised and globally distributed way. In the words of Eliot Higgins, the founder of Bellingcat, they are '… an intelligence agency for the people'[10].

What this means we do not yet know. One likely outcome is that there will be fewer places to hide nefarious, unethical or unfair practices. If a sufficiently motivated group of people decide that something should be investigated, they now have the means to access data, analyse it and share it cheaply and easily amongst themselves. I believe this is a social trend that will become more mainstream in the future. It will have significant consequences for how governments and business will govern themselves. They will have to become adept at being open about the decisions they are making, whilst also retaining enough secrecy to be able to function. This isn't a vision of utopia – it's an emerging reality. Organisations will need to fundamentally reset their expectations about what makes a good leader and how the performance of this leader should be recognised and acknowledged (clue: it is unlikely to be just about profit).

However, there is a note of caution here. As citizens become more empowered – through technology – responsibility increases too. One of the more regrettable trends during the Covid-19 pandemic has been that good, well-meaning people have shared well-presented and compelling but ultimately dangerous misinformation over social media. Unfortunately, some people act on this misinformation because it tells them something they want to believe, rather than what is happening. This has led to people not following official guidelines, increasing the risks to their own and others' health. Citizen science will need to be held to a higher standard, and post-Covid there will be greater emphasis on science to inform how we act in the world.

## A Science-Driven Post-Pandemic World

As I write this, a third wave of coronavirus has hit Germany; but even while the pandemic continues, one thing is clear: technology has been our saviour. Imagine for a moment being unable to send an email, to watch the news, or to video conference (and incidentally we should remember that this *is* still the case for some).

The disruptive ripples of Covid-19 will continue for decades. We do not yet know what the future will hold for us. We are certainly on a different global trajectory. This new world will reveal new opportunities, whilst closing off existing ones. Over the next few years, we will need to recover our lives, our livelihoods and our prospects. The scale of the challenge is simply unknown.

Every government will need to figure out economic recovery plans for their nation. This may be done in cooperation with other countries. Some of it will be inward looking – and may appear anti-cooperative and anti-business (increased taxation, trade tariffs, promotion of home-based competitors). Economic recovery should not undermine economic strength in the longer term. There may be a surge in nationalism and less international co-operation. However, recovery will need to build in future resilience, and international cooperation will be essential.

We will undoubtedly strive to prevent infectious disease from undermining our society and our economies in this way again. We may find that contact tracing becomes the norm and is extended to other transmissible diseases such as sexually transmitted infections and seasonal flu. This will require sharing of sensitive, private data.

Citizen trust is key. We will need to ensure that we set and adhere to standards throughout the design, evaluation, verification and implementation of such technologies. Trust in the fairness, privacy and security of data use will be critical; decision-making will need to be transparent and ethical. Unfortunately, citizen trust has already been eroded and if this continues, such a strategy may no longer be feasible.

We urgently need to implement standards – such as the IEEE's fairness framework or IBM's data ethics framework – and to increase the professionalisation of research and modelling software. We need to understand the basis of so-called algorithmic bias (meaning the bias of the algorithm itself, rather than bias or unfairness inherent in the underlying model that an algorithm is implementing).

In the UK, throughout the Covid-19 crisis, the British Computer Society have emphasised how user trust must be built on standards and professionalisation in the development and deployment of such capabilities. We must hope that government, at the national and local level, becomes highly competent in using data and models to develop fair, clear and beneficial policies, and to minimise disruption whilst keeping citizens safe.

The Covid-19 crisis has had profound impact on our values and our habits. These changes are two-fold. First, we have realised through necessity that for a large portion of the population, especially knowledge workers, it is possible to work effectively away from the office. This may instigate a long-term shift to valuing flexibility and freedom of working as part of selecting employers to work for. Second, in the short-term, the use of public transport may continue to be avoided or, at the least, only undertaken where necessary.

These changes to how we work and how we move around is leading to second-order effects: the expense of living in a city like London, New York or Paris no longer makes quite so much sense if you spend most of the time working from home. Couple that with the different experience that lockdown has on someone living in an over-crowded city apartment block compared to someone living in a rural property where the nearest neighbour is 100 metres away. Add to this that you inevitably get more for your money when buying outside of a city and, suddenly, country properties start to look more attractive.

A reduction in $CO_2$ emissions is likely to be a major, second order effect, of the changes left behind when Covid-19 subsides, as people move around less. Concurrently, we are likely to become far more reliant on technology companies to build and maintain the digital existence of entire countries.

The Covid-19 crisis has forced a dramatic reduction in air travel; it has forced the widespread use of communications and automation technologies that we have developed and created over the last 30 - 40 years, to allow some semblance of normality to continue – to keep us all connected in the virtual realm, even though we are not connected in the physical realm. As a solution to achieving $CO_2$ emission targets, a sagacious government may continue to encourage more working from home.

There will be major impacts on the oil industry – as there already have been – but it is essential for our survival that oil becomes less relevant. It is yesterday's story, and with the experiences through the lockdown there is an opportunity. We have learned how we can do things fundamentally differently, which also helps us achieve those targets.

We will need to use science to work our way through designing a post-Covid world just as we used science – from forecasting different scenarios to guide lockdown policies to the development of vaccines – to get ourselves through the pandemic. Science and technology have re-established themselves as our main means of responding to, and attempting to predict, what nature may throw at us.

We will need to continue to invest in building our cognitive advantage – enabled by AI and data science – by assisting humans in efficiently discovering solutions to problems. For example, to date over 22,000 scientific papers have been published on the Covid-19 virus. This is far more than any individual researcher, or a team of researchers, could study within a lifetime. And yet AI could significantly compress such a workload by automatically examining thousands of articles in days and by automatically generating summaries and recommendations for the benefit of the researchers.

## A World of Connected Technologies

For the past two decades three basic technologies have been converging: information technology, biotechnology and nanotechnology. Information technology has had the most visible impact on our lives, with the internet, mobile devices, communications technologies, artificial intelligence and cloud computing.

Nanotechnology is the invisible revolution in materials science and manufacturing that is allowing us to develop products with greater precision (microfluidics, carbon nanotubes), new properties (graphene) and new functionalities (miniaturised accelerometers and gyroscopes in drones, cameras and mobile phones).

Biotechnology is unleashing our creativity at the biological level and allowing us to directly observe, understand and intervene in complex biological pathways (e.g., synthetic biology technologies such as CRISPR) with truly profound prospects for our future. The point at which these three technologies are converging is at the sense → process → actuate level. Nanotechnology and biotechnology are making sensor technologies that are more accurate, smaller and cheaper. Information technology is enabling sensors to exchange data with other sensors without the need for human involvement, thus giving rise to the so-called Internet of Things.

The convergence of Info-Nano-Bio technologies is giving rise to a profound capability for us to, literally, program the code of life.

The Internet of Things is ushering in a new industrial revolution where our manufacturing systems will be integrated into a vast, interconnected network, creating real-time, hyper-connected feedback loops that drive intelligent action in the physical world.

Not only will this hyper-connected world of machines drive new opportunities for better, cheaper and faster goods, but it may also be a game-changer in mitigating climate change. For example, changing the throughput of a production line as a result of real-time measurements in $CO_2$ emissions in the local environment.

## Balkanisation of the Internet

We have talked about the accelerated pace of digitalisation due to Covid-19; another impact has been the effect on the global economy, revealing the fragility of the highly interlinked financial systems. The current technological trajectory is towards the Balkanisation of the internet, with a few large companies dominating. We need to find ways to increase the resilience of our global economy. Technology has a democratising effect. It creates the means for individuals to be more autonomous, with access to the information, the education and the context they need to make their own decisions.

The Electronic Frontiers Initiative says that the internet should always be free from government interference, because it doesn't work if people try to regulate it; but autonomy comes with accountability and personal responsibility; otherwise, society will remove that autonomy. Again, Covid-19 and contact-tracing apps are an example of this in action.

Our ability to communicate effectively with one another is reliant on the free movement of data around the world. However, there is a real risk that either the tech unicorns or the major superpowers will put boundaries in the cyber world to control the flow of data. A fibre might go underneath a sea which a nation claims as their territory. People are recognising that control of data gives a soft power in a geopolitical context. Technology enables lots of wonderful things, but the policies of the big tech companies and governments are often counter to that.

From a cognitive advantage perspective this is a very important part of the environment to understand. In whatever way this potential Balkanisation might pan out, it is essential to continually understand how we might need to pivot, or respond, or possibly even intervene, to prevent some of these effects being detrimental to the organisation. We need to have situational awareness of how the hardware and software of the internet is changing, and what the impact might be on our position in the environment. It is not just about hardware and physical data banks and physical cables; it is also about the standards used. China is emerging as a massive cyberpower, and at the moment they use Western languages: C++, Python, etc. – English-derived programming languages. The OSI (Open Standards Interconnection) stack that defines all the standards of the internet is under question as China brings in its own standards. Companies like Huawei are the main force for changes in line with China-derived data standards.

For a long time in the West, we have been privileged in that we have set the standards and the rest of the world followed. That world is changing, and it is shifting to the East. We need to understand the potential impact of that, and to be prepared. This isn't something that only the tech unicorns or governments need to worry about. As more companies, organisations and government departments become dependent on data to allow them to offer the best possible experiences to their customers or their citizens, a new standard on the internet will have a far more significant impact. Making sense of an operating environment that is built on standards written in a foreign language would create a significant cognitive *dis*advantage.

There are still many organisations that exist as a hybrid between paper-based, manual systems and data-driven systems, and without a great deal of automation. We are still in that post-industrial no-man's land between a full knowledge economy and an industrial economy. This is not sustainable. It is an essential matter of survival that these organisations change, by becoming more data-savvy, by understanding how their environment is changing, and how they need to change to keep up with it.

In terms of the world economy, we are still coming out of the industrial age, where big machines and mass transport are essential drivers of the economy. The fundamental, basic ingredient that literally fuelled the entire global economy was oil. Now as we move into an information age, data is the fundamental raw ingredient that fuels the knowledge economies, and these knowledge economies will become more and more central. Human time and effort will increasingly be spent on cerebral activity rather than on mechanical-manual tasks, as robotics take these over.

## Digitalisation and Virtualisation

The digitalisation of our world has accelerated through the Covid-19 lockdown. We are living through an extremely fascinating – although grim – time, from an anthropological point of view. Our use of technology to facilitate virtual work and co-ordination of projects has significantly increased through necessity. That is not going to go away. We were already on a trajectory to existing in a cyber world as much as a physical world, and the global pandemic has accelerated that process.

As we transition more into virtual, digital worlds there will be less need for people to physically get together to be productive and creative. With autonomous transport and robotics, fewer humans will be needed for traditional industries such as agriculture and transportation. These technologies will continue to mature and become mainstream.

In this cyber, digital world we will generate increasing volumes of data, either directly or indirectly, just by existing; and that data has value for people who want to influence us, or to sell to us. Our attention is valuable, and influencing our beliefs has a wide range of benefits for a wide range of people.

As data drives the global knowledge economy, access to good data – clean and relevant – will drive the activities of an organisation. This creates an entirely new marketplace.

The first era of Big Data, which we are still in, is one where we recognise the value of data, but we are struggling to realise that value. The second wave for Big Data, which we are moving into, is far more sophisticated, with most data analysis done by machines and learning algorithms; humans may only be involved to oversee the correct performance of machines. We are likely to find ourselves composing analytical efforts and doing less of it ourselves.

'While the rest of the world is living in 2019, Singapore seems to be in 2119'[11]. Whether such a bold statement still holds true at the end of 2020, with the Covid-19 pandemic accelerating the world's digitalisation, remains to be seen. However, one thing is clear: the Singaporean government are taking the smart city concept seriously. A smart city is one that uses data collected from huge numbers of sensors that form part of the Internet of Things.

Analysis of this data reveals insights into the status and performance of the city's assets, resources and services. For example, sensory data from buildings can tell us about internal temperature, occupancy levels, water usage, and so on. On the road, sensors continually detect pollution levels and traffic congestion. Water-based sensors monitor water quality and flow sensors monitor usage. The output from these devices were stitched together to yield a total understanding of the state of a city.

Turning this sensor output into the awareness and adaptability needed to enable the smooth running of the city requires specialised analysis of the data. Singapore's Urban Redevelopment Authority has created a department – called Virtual Singapore – to reconstruct the whole city in extreme detail. The software – developed by the French company Dassault Systemes – allows users to visualise parts of the city as a 3D map overlain with real-time data. This 3D virtual representation of the city is accessible by the public and private sectors. It is a national asset available to all, to help with the development of this smart city.

Knowing how to harness vast amounts of data to aid with understanding and, crucially, developing policies and actions, requires the ability to model complex systems. Singapore is also pioneering in this area. In early January 2017, the Centre for Liveable Cities (another Singaporean government department) ran a workshop with participants from across the world, titled *Harnessing Complexity and Data Science to Develop Urban Solutions for Singapore*.

The conclusion of the workshop was quite clear, 'Rather than seeking to isolate problems and to provide targeted solutions, thereby inadvertently creating silos, policymakers need to acknowledge that cities are complex adaptive systems and take a more holistic approach towards planning or urban growth and development'[12]. The Singaporean government took this advice seriously and, in September 2019, announced that all 150,000 of their civil servants would be given a working knowledge in, and understanding of, complexity science.

The smart city concept is fundamentally dependent on data. As such, data will be a highly valued commodity that is essential for the running of any organisation, and essential for the running of any city and society. Singapore is furthest down the trajectory towards a true digital society (with Estonia close behind), in terms of maximising the use of data in the running of the city.

There is a privacy trade-off we need to be aware of. The Singaporean people seem to accept that being safer – whether from Covid, or from crime – being cleaner, being more efficient, with the positive impact on levels of pollution and fluidity of transportation, is worth the impact on privacy.

Singapore is an exemplar of what the world might look like in 5-10 years' time, for better or worse; there is a fundamental necessity to keep data flowing, because the civil systems – electricity, smart highways, the whole smart city – are fundamentally dependent on the timely and continuous flow of data. As soon as data stops, everything will grind to a halt.

Whereas previously countries have fought wars over oil – because they recognised that their economy, their society, required continual, reliable and fair-priced access to oil – in the future, with continued digitalisation, data will have that key strategic importance. But only when it has been collected, understood, analysed and acted on at a speed that is relevant and impactful.

## The Increased Meaning of Trust

We don't yet know what the lasting effects of Covid-19 will be, on ways of working, on how we interact as a society. Until early 2020 we had very little understanding of how rapidly society could change in this way, and how quickly our view of privacy and freedom could alter in the face of an external threat – in this case a pandemic, but we have seen similar changes in response to terrorism. We have been willing to give up these things in some measure in exchange for safety; and we have seen how in Singapore the exchange is for efficiency and convenience as well as security.

Ultimately this is not just about government, it is about the use of data extending into industry and impacting citizens. Trust and transparency are vital subjects, two sides of the same conversation. Trust is knowing that when someone promises to do something, they won't do any different. If we understand why we are giving access to our information and we understand what we are getting in return, there is an equitable social contract, and both parties expect that contract to be upheld. Transparency is the ability to test whether that trust is valid. Has the agreement been followed? With GDPR and other legislative instruments, we are addressing the tip of the iceberg. As we move into an increasingly data-rich world, the bar will be raised for companies to take more responsibility for their actions.

Governments have traditionally been several steps behind industry, because they have been less involved in pioneering new uses of technology. As companies like Facebook bump up against privacy issues, this has caused governments to bring in legislation as a reaction. In the future it won't be acceptable for governments to just follow industry. Governments will want to use data from their citizens in ways that industry either doesn't have the legal authority to do, or wouldn't have interest in doing, unless paid to do so by government. There is a need for public dialogue and defining things in the public interest. We need sagacious decisions about how organisations and government departments shape the environment.

There is a real paradox with Singapore. On the one hand Lee Hsien Loong is quite belligerent, quite forceful, and therefore his altruism is questionable, but the bigger picture is that he has done a lot of good for Singapore: improved international reputation, reduced crime, provided better access to healthcare. There is increasing encroachment on people's privacy. The Singapore government has a huge and increasing appetite for data. They may do well to study Sweden whose citizens have accepted less privacy in return for increased safety (although it should be noted that the Swedish government is strictly held to account for its actions as part of a well-established and working democracy).

China and India are on the same trajectory, seeking far more access to data about what their citizens are doing, where they are, who they are talking to. Trust and transparency are a huge issue, because if a government doesn't get this right, if there is a breakdown in trust, then that has serious ramifications for individual citizens, and for the country. If data is essential to the safe and effective running of the city, or a country, but there is a breakdown in access to that data because people are motivated to restrict its flow, there can be enormous unintended consequences of getting it wrong.

I don't believe governments properly understand trust and transparency, because – as I said at the beginning of this chapter – the world is changing faster than governments can comprehend.

## Diversifying our Economy

The fragility of the global system played out perfectly in Covid-19. At the very top level, the field of economics is about supply and demand, and about human behaviour in trading. In terms of the window of viability, too much efficiency can make the system brittle, and with too much diversity nothing useful gets done. The 2008 banking crisis was a classic example of brittleness, and over-efficiency, overdependency on a handful of currencies to value all other currencies. Alternative currencies have an important role in building more resilience into the global system. Interestingly, Bitcoin followed quite soon after, and we don't fully understand how that is going to play out.

With Covid-19, China was the first nation impacted, and the country went into lockdown. That created a massive dearth of supply, since most developed economies are dependent on China as a supplier. There was a big impact on the financial market, and then as the virus spread globally, demand massively dampened, for goods, and for materials, and for oil.

The global system is dependent on oil to keep the economy moving – with corresponding impact on the environment; but the pandemic has perturbed the demand-supply relationship, and at this point we don't know how this is going to play out. Every government has had to step in with a massive recovery package – and we don't know how the consequent debt will impact moving into the future.

We have designed our global systems to be much too simplified, much too efficient. We link barrels of oil production to valuation of currencies, for example. We are outside the window of viability; in that we have streamlined efficiency beyond long-term sustainability. More adaptability is required to create more resilience.

One of the conversations going on now is about diversifying currencies post-Covid by the establishment of more microeconomies, where big international cities – including Manchester and Birmingham and Edinburgh, and Glasgow and Cardiff alongside London in the UK – have their own currencies, their own microeconomies. Such initiatives could learn from the long-standing micro currencies used in cities such as Bristol (the Bristol pound) and Liverpool (the Colu).

In the 1970s the economist Schumacher wrote a book *Small is Beautiful* about microeconomies. His view is that we need to have a much more locally sensitised view of supply and demand, rather than overdependency on globalisation; with globalisation we get efficiencies, lower prices, and so on, but the risk is brittleness. If we are to move our economy back into the window of viability, we need to diversify our economic system.

Cryptocurrencies and alternative currencies and breaking down state-level economies into international city-level economies might be key factors as the global economy evolves over the next decade. The fact that Tesla – the world's most valuable car manufacturer – now accepts Bitcoin payments, could well be the catalyst for more widespread adoption of these alternative currencies. This could fundamentally re-write the rule book on our global economic system. It may pave the way for Schumacher's vision for smaller, more localised economies.

This chapter has considered some of the main trends that are already shaping our world and that will continue to do so in ways that we do not yet know. The challenge for the leadership of an organisation is this: how do we develop the ability to *thrive* in a world that is changing faster than we can learn about it? How do we make the right investments to position ourselves to be in the right place at the right time? How do we build the means to act with deep insight and confidence routinely and proactively in this vastly complex and dynamic operating environment? And how do we do that at pace and yet do so ethically and responsibly?

Building and maintaining a cognitive advantage gives the means for an organisation to understand, harness and shape complex environments.

# Chapter 3
# Autonomy and Cognition

*'intelligence is the ability to adapt to change'*[13]

Stephen Hawking (apocryphal)

If we are to design AI to augment our ability to manage, and get ahead, in an increasingly turbulent and uncertain world, then we need to understand how humans think, what we are good at and what we are not so good at. Until we do that, our application of AI to help us may be somewhat haphazard.

We should also have an appreciation of why we think at all. This isn't simply rhetoric. Understanding why cognition is such a key ingredient for survival and reproduction in nature may help us engineer AI that works well for us, as individuals and for our institutions and organisations. So, to begin to understand cognition, let us consider a theory of how complex systems – living cells, people, societies – endure.

## Autonomy

autonomy (noun):

*'freedom from external control and influence'*[14]

Historically autonomy has referred to nations that have the right to self-govern and to set their own laws. These autonomous regions established their own identity (for example, a national flag) and their leaders determined how the country should be run (hopefully in a fair and just manner). However, autonomy does not mean self-determination.

Autonomy is not truly possible for any system. A nation may have its own identity, its own customs, but it also seeks to trade with other nations. The establishing of trade agreements is a cooperative act, and a degree of compromise is inevitable. It is the same with peace treaties. Hence, the use of the word autonomy here refers to a system that can maintain an identity, perceive and react to changes in its environment, and that can persist.

Current research into general artificial intelligence aims to create machines that exhibit autonomy. That is not our focus here. I am interested in the role that machines (AI) could play in helping existing autonomous systems (humans) become more capable. To begin to design how AI and humans can work together effectively, at scale, we need to understand the basic components of an autonomous system. Fortunately, such a concept already exists: the theory of autopoiesis (self-production and self-maintenance).

## A Scheme for a Minimal Autonomous System

Autopoiesis is a Greek word meaning self-producing. It is a phrase used by two Chilean neurobiologists, Francisco Varela and Humberto Maturana, in 1974, to describe the intrinsic property that distinguishes a living system from a non-living system. They observed that a living system can continually maintain itself, repair itself and reproduce; it doesn't need an external agent to come in and fix it. It might be dependent on the availability of resources in its environment, but the transformation of those materials into a form that an autopoietic system needs to repair and reproduce is undertaken within itself. This self-sufficiency gives rise to a degree of autonomous behaviour that distinguishes the autopoietic system from its environment. In other words, an autopoietic system is identifiable.

*'An autopoietic machine is a machine organized (defined as a unity) as a network of processes of production (transformation and destruction) of components that produces the components which: (i) through their interactions and transformations continuously regenerate and realize the network of processes (relations) that produced them; and (ii) constitute it (the machine) as a concrete unity in the space in which they (the components) exist by specifying the topological domain of its realization as such a network.'*[15]

Maturana & Varela, The Realization of the Living, 1980.

It is a beautiful idea to explain why certain forms of organised systems persist and others don't: that the systems that persist have this quality of being self-producing.

A good example of an autopoietic system is a basic living cell (Figure 1 is an abstract depiction of the main functions required for a biological cell to endure). The internal reactions in a cell produce the components that form its membrane. This membrane separates the internal components and processes from the environment, whilst allowing key nutrients in and expunging waste products out. This changes the behaviour of the internal reactions that created the membrane in the first place. There is a bottom-up cause (chemical reactions producing the components that constitute the membrane) and a top-down effect (the membrane changes the availability and the flow of materials, thus changing the internal reactions). This circularity creates a unity, a whole that is a minimal living cell. Of course, the actual mechanics of a real biological cell rely on complex molecular machinery, but we don't need to go into that here. For now, this is an example of the minimal operation of an autonomous entity. Take any of these bottom-up or top-down processes away and you no longer have a system that can maintain itself.

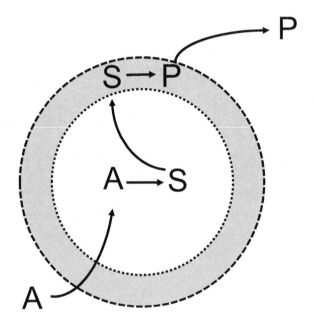

*Figure 1. An illustration of Luisi's schematic of a minimal autopoietic cell where a substrate entity (A) produces the product (S) which links to other S entities to form a boundary which encapsulates the A->S reaction. Over time S decays to the waste product (P) leaving a hole in the boundary which is repaired by another S molecule generated from the internal reaction.*

Why am I discussing autopoiesis? There are two reasons: firstly, humans are autopoietic systems (albeit incredibly complex ones) and the autopoietic process of maintaining ourselves is why we need cognitive capabilities; and secondly, autopoiesis gives us a succinct description of an autonomous system. As I will go on to discuss, any form of organisation – whether that is a football team, a company, a government or an entire country – consists of processes for maintaining itself.

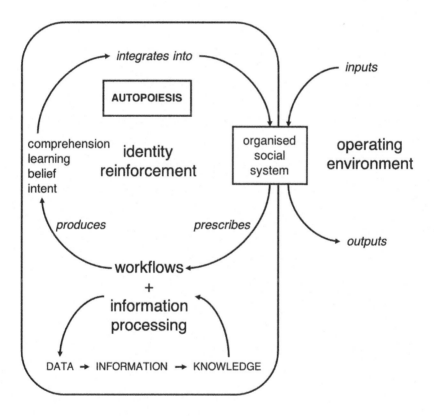

*Figure 2. A conceptual diagram of an autopoietic system as a series of processes where data is transformed into knowledge which drives the work required to maintain the operation of the organisation.*

This idea was proposed by Niklas Luhmann in his book *Theory of Society*, which was based on the theory of autopoiesis. He said that individuals have their own identity in society, they seek to maintain that identity (their social standing), and most seek to reproduce themselves. He also extended the idea to institutions. The institution is an autopoietic system and the components that maintain it are the individuals who work for that institution. Of course, people and institutions – just like biological cells – do not exist in a vacuum. Luhmann said that society is no different from a biological cell. A biological cell maintains its identity in its environment (and there is a distinction between the biological cell and the environment) and so it is with people, communities and companies.

The components and the elements that we use to maintain our identity are different, but the organising concept is the same. Whereas in the biological sense we might talk about chemicals and molecules, in a social sense we talk about ideas, beliefs and group membership. Consider Figure 2.

An organisation is a distinct entity in an environment. Every company has a name, a mission, a purpose, and these distinguish this company from others. It also pursues a path of survival – self-production and self-maintenance. The way organisations respond to the environment – and the thinking underpinning that response – is based on reinforcing identity and position in the marketplace.

One of the functions of cognition is to comprehend whether the organisation's identity is being maintained. If there is a perceived risk that the organisation's goals will not be met, then the organisation either needs to reinvent itself or protect itself. Either way, comprehension drives action. Cognition requires information, ability to process that information, and ability to act.

How an individual thinks, what they believe, and the interactions they have with fellow humans or with the environment, are based on a perception of themselves and their position in the environment and in society: who they are and what they stand for. In other words, their perception of their identity; and how they can act in their environment.

In the future, AI will be managed by policy and legislation, in the same way that societies are managed by policy and legislation. That is the extent to which AI will persist and exist. The credo of a company informs the ability of a board to make sagacious decisions, and this extends to AI also. When we are setting that policy for how our AI will operate, and the rules of law by which our AI will go out into the world and behave on our behalf, we need to recognise that these are an instantiation of our identity as an organisation – how we want to be perceived within our environment and positioned in our ecosystem.

## Window of Viability

The California-based ecologist, Dr. Robert Ulanowicz, published a paper in 1983, where he used the phrase *window of viability* to define a limited state space – a Goldilocks zone – where an ecological system maximises its sustainability, by being sufficiently diverse and simultaneously sufficiently efficient. Diversity (or variety) introduces important redundancy into the system, thus allowing it to respond to shocks and perturbations from the environment. Efficiency ensures that the system can effectively use resources to maintain itself. As such, the optimal sustainability is a balance between redundancy and efficiency.

In more recent times, Ulanowicz co-authored a paper with Bernard Lietaer (a world-renowned ex-currency trader and academic) who used the model to explain the banking crisis that rocked the global economy in 2008. Lietaer & Ulanowicz suggested that the global banking system was too efficient – which they described as 'brittle' – and consequently ill-equipped to deal with unexpected changes. The international banking system lacked redundancy, having a limited number of currencies. Subsequently, their 2010 paper concludes that the world needs a greater variety of currencies. Lietaer was a strong advocate for local currencies.

From my own work on computer simulations of autopoietic systems, I discovered that robust autopoietic systems – those that could withstand sudden changes in the environment – were those that could adapt the rate at which information and materials was exchanged with the environment. If an autopoietic system had too little exposure to the environment, and therefore most of the information and materials that it was processing were produced from within, then – over time – this led to a reduction in the diversity of information and materials within the system. Such systems did not adapt well to sudden changes in the environment.

Conversely, my simulations also revealed that too much exposure to the environment (again, in the form of an exchange of materials and information) meant that the integrity of the autopoietic system was compromised to the point where it was no longer distinguishable from the environment. It had, quite simply, lost the ability to construct and maintain an identity.

All organisations – companies, governments, universities, and so on – persist within a window of viability. Indeed, we can think of ourselves and the groups we form with other people, as doing likewise.

For a system to be able to maintain itself within this window of viability, when change occurs it must either adjust its internal processes, components or structures; or somehow shape the environment in a way that allows it to continue to operate.

Our ability to act is shaped by our innate abilities and the state of the environment, and – in acting – we shape the environment. The key is to ensure that we are shaping the environment in our favour.

To illustrate this, let me re-tell the example used by Wheeler, of the humble earthworm. As a worm digs a tunnel in soil, its secretions reinforce the structural integrity of the tunnel. This not only allows the worm to move more efficiently through the soil, but it also provides the space required for the worm to digest its food. Through its own action (secretions) the worm has shaped its environment (stable tunnels) in a way that allows it to absorb important nutrients from the soil that are critical to its wellbeing. There is a feedback loop from the worm (the autopoietic system) into the environment (the soil) and back to the worm (the space to manoeuvre). The effect of its output affects its input. There is, if you like, an operational coupling between the system and its environment; and the worm's survival is fundamentally dependent on that coupling.

Hence an autopoietic system must be well-fitted to its operating environment, and ideally there is a co-dependency between the environment and the system itself. Shaping the environment is about optimising this operational coupling.

Being able to interact with the environment is fundamental to a cognitive/learning process. This is where anticipation comes in, and hypothesis testing. First, we attempt to make sense of our environment, and to attach meaning to it, but then we need to test that understanding to prove whether it is correct. Second, we use whatever ability we have, to act in the environment – or in a simulated model of the environment – to test our hypothesis.

This is complex. For a global company, the number of interactions it has with its external environment is immeasurable – for a human, at least. Millions of interactions every second, with a corresponding number of data points to understand. Why should a company or a government department invest the time and effort to make sense of all the interactions that occur in an organisation every day?

When we aspire to shape an environment, we need to understand the causal architecture of that environment. Until we have insight into the underlying causal flow that drives the behaviour of an environment, it is difficult to understand the most efficacious way for us exert effort into that environment so that we endure. Therefore, we learn and we reason. As I discuss in the next chapter, we reason based on an understanding of cause and effect. We learn about cause-and-effect from the day we are born, and we never stop.

So far, I have talked about biological cells and earthworms. But what does this have to do with using AI to gain a competitive edge? Humans have evolved to be very complex autopoietic systems. If we strip away our sophisticated and complex actions and behaviours, what is left is a basic urge to survive and reproduce. This urge to endure manifests itself in us as individuals and collectively as a society. We strive to have an identity in our social groups. Companies strive to endure. As do governments. This innate need is universal to all living systems. So, if we are to engineer AI to help us endure, then we need to understand and explore the fundamental mechanism by which all living systems endure. The theory of autopoiesis gives us a foundation for this understanding and exploration.

## Cognition

cognition (noun):

*'The mental action or process of acquiring knowledge and understanding through thought, experience, and the senses'*[16]

Psychologists understand cognition as information processing. We receive information from our senses – the input – and process it in some way. When we act, that is an output from the system. As we process information – as we perceive – it can be helpful to think of ascending a hierarchy: the raw signals (the data) at the bottom and then, as we add structure to that data, we create information.

Information describes what our senses have collected. To do this we have to recognise what we are seeing, hearing, feeling or smelling. As we understand how that information links to our previous experience, we construct knowledge. Knowledge represents what we have learned. With knowledge we know how to do something with the information we have received.

Knowledge gives us an explanation of what we are perceiving, and, from that, we reach an understanding of why we are perceiving what we are perceiving. As we add context to knowledge – *the object is coming towards me* – we determine what to do about it. We use our experience of a similar previous event to make a good decision.

Jennifer Rowley – building on Russell Ackoff's earlier work - calls this the *Wisdom Hierarchy* (see Figure 3) and she succinctly explains the relationship between the levels in the hierarchy: '… information is defined in terms of data, knowledge in terms of information, and wisdom in terms of knowledge'[17]. Information and Knowledge process events that have already occurred. Wisdom processes possible events that may occur. Hence, whilst Information and Knowledge can tell us everything, we need to know about what is currently happening, we need Wisdom to decide on the best action to take.

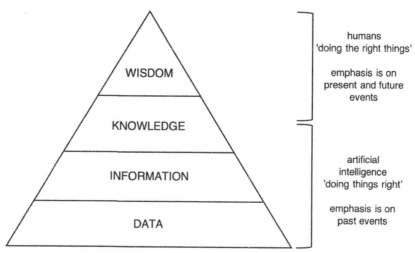

*Figure 3. The Wisdom Hierarchy concept suggests that adding structure, context and meaning to raw data can yield insights from which we can learn and apply that learning to future events. Inspired by Russell Ackoff's 'From Data to Wisdom'.*

When we are perceiving a more complex environment – where there is ambiguity and uncertainty resulting from new and unexpected things happening, and/or the speed at which things are happening – the best action to take becomes less certain. Somewhat perversely, highly complex changes in the environment tend to elicit actions that we feel are riskier. The stakes are higher, or, at the least, we believe they are.

The ordering of this hierarchy illustrates a reduction in the number of entities that are processed at each level. That is, a significantly higher number of individual entities need to be processed at the Data level compared to the Wisdom level. As such, very fast processing of information is required at the lower levels of this hierarchy, whereas speed becomes less critical towards the top of the hierarchy. As such, I propose that we should primarily focus AI on doing most of the heavy lifting, to progress up the hierarchy from Data to Information to Knowledge. Then humans can focus more on the application of knowledge to determine the best course of action. This topic is revisited in Chapter 4 and 5.

## The Perception-Action Loop

Psychologists have a theory that we perceive our environment through our ability to act in it. We interpret what is happening in our environment through the lens of how we may respond. That belief in how we may act, and our intent to act, influence how we perceive the environment. Our actions are determined by our pursuit of a goal: finding food or mates, avoiding danger, or being the market leader. Whatever it might be, our actions are directed at pursuing that goal, and that intent shapes our perception of our environment, which is also constantly changing.

The perception-action loop begins by taking in and processing information from the environment; then comparing that information to what was expected; then shaping our actions as a result. The goal provides the all-important context for perceiving differences between expectation and reality in the environment.

If we combine the wisdom hierarchy with the Perception and Action loop, we create a circular flow as depicted in Figure 4.

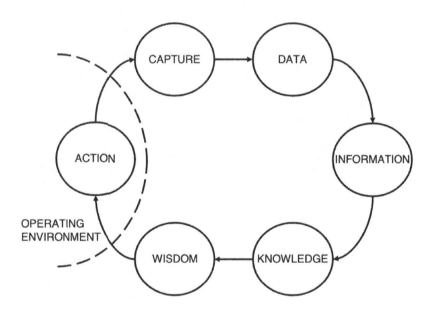

*Figure 4. Wisdom hierarchy applied to a Perception-Action loop.*

As and when new information comes to us, we go through a Perception-Action loop. The environment is constantly observed, and as something changes, effort is made to make sense of that change (perceive) and contextualise it: Is this something we care about? Does it affect the pursuit of the goal? Then comes the decision of how to act.

Perception-Action loops are useful as a conceptual framework for thinking about how to design an organisation so that it can continually adapt to its environment. The perception-action loop is a biological, scientific explanation of how humans learn.

A similar concept has been developed by John Boyd and is known as OODA loops: Observe, Orient, Decide, Act. Boyd suggested that it is important to focus on the information that is most relevant, at that moment in time, to the prosecution of a goal, then to put that information into context, and then make the most appropriate decision.

OODA loops conform to the *action-influenced perception* school of thought. Action-influenced perception is a form of anticipation. We are not only anticipating what might happen next, we are also preparing for how we will act. The subject of our focus becomes more prominent, more colourful, more detailed as we pivot more of our information processing capacity in concentrating on it. For example, if I throw a tennis ball to you then your ability to catch it (and achieve the necessary hand-eye coordination) is enabled through action-influenced perception.

OODA loops are a generalised framework for understanding decision-making in relation to the environment. Boyd developed this idea for use in military situations, and it has clear applicability to cognitive advantage, and in systematically designing an organisation where everyone – whether at individual, team or organisational level – is operating on an OODA loop and is consciously aware that they are doing so. In this way they can prosecute their goal in a rapidly changing environment. OODA loops reflect the value of having a vast appetite for information and understanding how the environment is changing.

The cognitive enterprise (which I describe in Chapter 8) is a system of distributed and collaborative Perception-Action loops – or OODA loops – augmented by artificial intelligence.

## Learning from Others

Ralph Stacey, a social scientist, was interested in how people really behave in organisations. When humans work together, whether one-to-one, or at scale, how do we make decisions? What drives behaviour in an organisation? He developed a concept called Complex Responsive Processes and said that all human interaction is a complex responsive process.

We carry around in our heads a predictive model of the world, from our perspective, and when we have a conversation with another human, by the very nature of that conversation we are revealing aspects of our predictive model to each other. We are not always aware of this because we wrap it up in language, but we share something of our beliefs or our knowledge as we have a conversation; and as a result, we learn from each other, and our internal model of the world changes or is reinforced.

Mary Parker Follett wrote about this 100 years ago. She said conversations tend to have two types of themes. The first is conversations where there is a differentiation process going on – for example with brainstorming – where we are exploring, expanding out concepts, trying to understand something and be creative and see all possibilities. These conversations are about absorbing new ideas and options and then challenging our beliefs, knowledge and understanding of things. We can think of this as a spiral, starting in the middle and expanding outwards. Examples of differentiation are asking simple questions, such as, 'How was your day?'

The second type of conversation is integration, where the exploration is complete and the next step is, 'What does that mean to me? Am I going to do anything about this? Does this change anything? Has it changed my belief about something?'

Differentiation, that explosion of knowledge and exploration, is sense-making, trying to figure something out; and the integration process is meaning-making. It is the, 'So what?'. Follett articulates this beautifully. She describes how people need to be in small teams to allow this constant, free-flowing differentiation and integration, because that is the way people learn, and that is the way groups of people can change their environment.

Follett showed great foresight in writing about this in the early 20$^{th}$ century, when the rest of the thinking world was buying into Taylorism (Frederick Taylor's management science and *time and method* studies). Taylorism was industrial efficiency at the expense of individuality with the unintentional side effect of dehumanising work. It was very efficient, very profitable, to take a team of people and get them all to do separate and highly repetitive work to give maximum shareholder return, but this allowed no craft skills to be taught or developed. Follett was strongly against this; she said it was destroying humans, destroying creativity.

Ralph Stacey, using modern social science concepts and frameworks, has brought her ideas back to life. He uses complexity science as the basis for spotting when a significant change is happening in the environment. This is essential for reacting before anyone else can, or in fact just to survive. Follett talks about differentiation and integration; Ralph Stacey calls it complex responsive processes; psychologists and sociologists refer to it as a dialectic process. New information, in whatever form, leads to learning something new.

Difference is important, and dialectic processes allow us to benefit from difference. This is fundamental to cognitive advantage. There is an intrinsic drive for any form of living system – whether biological, or a man-made construct such as an organisation – to stay alive and maintain its identity. This self-sustaining process – autopoiesis – is a dialectic process; learning and complex responsive processes are the mechanics of how to stay within the window of viability. These are the detailed processes of keeping pace with the external environment.

When we come on to talk about the cognitive enterprise, the design principles of the cognitive enterprise are about augmenting highly effective dialectic processes throughout the entire organisation, at every level, and outside of the organisation with the environment, with partners and customers, etc. This is obvious when stated but codifying this – making it part of what we do daily and explicitly recognising that that is what we are doing – means putting effort into measuring it and doing it well.

Self-awareness is essential for long term success. Every organisation, every individual, generates a lot of data, just through normal day to day activity. Increasing our awareness of this is key to harnessing the possibilities of future technology. Advertising companies, the big platforms such as Facebook and Google, are making use of this data, but as human beings we have a long way to go. There are minor tools now to benefit us, tell us how much screen time we had this week, or an Apple Watch telling us it is time to get up out of the chair, but, unless we explicitly seek it out, we are oblivious to the wealth of data that exists. It is the same at an organisational level, and therefore making the dialectic learning process explicit, recognising the potential for a deliberate conversation that is going on all the time, everywhere, allows us to harness that potential, to get good at it.

This is critical because unless we are doing that sense-making and meaning-making, and doing it effectively, and doing it better than the competition, we will never be able to develop a cognitive advantage.

## Autopoiesis and the Cognitive Enterprise

Autopoiesis provides the theoretical backdrop to the cognitive enterprise, which we come on to later in the book. I propose a design for an organisation, and a template for how an organisation can build a cognitive advantage.

The design is based on the premise of accepting the theory of autopoiesis, accepting the idea of building the organisation through continual monitoring of the environment, testing changes in that environment against the identity and what the organisation stands for – its purpose, its goals – and then deciding whether to intervene in that environment, because there is a difference between where the environment ideally should be, from the organisation's standpoint, and where it is.

The structural coupling of the autopoietic system with the environment – as defined by its informational and operational limits – will be key to leveraging the right action. The processes underpinning autopoiesis are cognitive functions.

By isolating and understanding cognition as information processing – as we have done in this chapter – we can begin to engineer AI that fulfils its own complete information processing cycle, whilst helping us (humans) handle the processing and interpreting of more complex and ambiguous information.

# Chapter 4
# Artificial Intelligence

*'I propose to consider the question, "Can machines think?"'*[18]

Alan Turing

## What is Artificial Intelligence?

With those opening words to his 1950 paper, *Computing Machinery and Intelligence*, Alan Turing laid the first foundation stone in the field of Artificial Intelligence. He goes on to describe an experiment, called The Imitation Game, in which an interrogator asks questions of two participants who are in different rooms, and neither of whom are visible to the interrogator.

Through a series of questions, the interrogator is to determine if a participant is a human or a machine (as a curious aside, he first introduces the thought experiment using the example of an interrogator determining if a participant is a man or a woman). The participants can only communicate with the interrogator by some indirect means such as a typed message and so there are no visual cues. If the interrogator cannot determine, with confidence, the nature of the participant then, Turing argued, a machine could passably demonstrate intelligent behaviour.

He predicted that by the year 2000 a machine would be so advanced that a human interrogator would only have a 70% chance of correctly guessing if they were conversing with a human or a machine after 5 minutes of questioning. Turing's Imitation Game became known as the Turing Test. It was a brilliant piece of original thinking that set out a means to evaluate an artificial intelligence, should we ever have the means to develop one.

As it happened, and as Turing cites in his paper, two of his contemporaries, Norbert Wiener, working with his work on dynamic control in electronic systems (Wiener became known as the Father of Cybernetics), and Claude Shannon, the creator of Information Theory (which introduced us to digital information), had recently proposed theories that, between all three, made plausible the idea of developing an electronic brain. They were not the first.

A decade earlier, Walter Pitts and Warren McCulloch demonstrated how artificial neurons could perform logical functions such as AND and OR – fundamental information processing building blocks of all computers. Their work would later be described as the first neural network.

Following on from the confluence of Shannon, Turing and Wiener's work, funding for AI research started flowing and, apart from a six year *Winter of AI* during 1974-1980, important developments were made in machine vision (Gerald Sussman, Adolfo Guzman, David Waltz and Patrick Winston), semantic networks (Ross Quillan, Roger Schank), Joseph Weizenbaum's ELIZA, the world's first chatterbot, and WABOT-1, the world's first intelligent robot, developed by a team at Waseda University in Japan, that could interact with its environment through picking up objects.

Early research into AI faced one serious impediment. Lack of computing power and capacity. Whether it was in machine vision, or in natural language processing, researchers understood the tools at their disposal were woefully inadequate to the task, in information processing speed and in 'memory' to store programs and data of a size that would be required. So, instead, they developed simplified models as proofs-of-concept, but little more. Unfortunately, in the early 1970s, this realisation led to severe cuts in the funding of AI research. The technology was not there. The data was not there. Regardless of the cooling effect that Marvin Minsky and Seymour Papert's book called *Perceptrons* may have had (they mathematically proved that neural networks *at that time* had very limited functionality in the real world, but they were subsequently proven wrong) there was also a simple, stark reality: the world was not yet ready.

Fast forward to the second decade of the 21$^{st}$ century. We had an abundance of data and a seemingly unlimited computing capacity. Claims of AI that could pass the Turing Test quickly began to emerge.

Eugene Goostman was a 13-year-old boy from Ukraine, except he wasn't. Eugene was, in fact, a chatbot which convinced a judge that it was a human. Developed by a team of programmers – Vladimir Veselov, Eugene Demchenko and Sergey Ulasen – Eugene competed in a series of organised Turing Test contests in 2005, 2008 and 2012. However, it was in 2014 that Eugene passed the threshold – through a re-interpretation of Turing's 70% chance of correctly guessing the nature of the conversant – by convincing 33% of the human judges that Goostman was, in fact, human. However, strong criticism from experts such as Gary Marcus (one of the more grounded and foresighted researchers currently in the field of AI) pointed out that a piece of software that has been programmed to misdirect and deflect questions from a human does not represent an artificial intelligence.

In 2018 the media breathlessly announced that Google had succeeded at the Turing Test. Google's Duplex – a more advanced form of chatbot that could orally converse with a human – heralded genuine artificial intelligence so it was claimed. Google's Duplex performs a simple task: you ask it to 'Book me a table at Bubba's Big Fish Bonanza for Friday night' and it will phone the restaurant and converse with the Restaurant Manager, even to the degree of choosing different times and dates. Not only does Google Duplex hold a useful conversation with a human, but it's also imitating a human by adding in pauses, stuttering, and so on. It takes the 'Imitation Game' to the next level. Now, apart from the ethical issues that this raises (for example, is it fair to *not* inform the human receiving the phone call that they are conversing with a machine?) the important point here is that Google Duplex is *imitating* a human to complete a task. That is not the same as saying that it has human-level intelligence. This, I believe, is where there is either wilful ignorance (to make a compelling news headline) or a genuine misunderstanding of what the Turing Test can usefully tell us about machine intelligence. Experts such as Gary Marcus know how to trip up an AI and they can quickly identify the failings of machine intelligence offerings in having a credible level of understanding of our world such that they can demonstrate a near-human level of intelligence.

So, developing an AI that has a common-sense model of the world that they share with us is one challenge. But what about new experiences and random events? Humans use creativity, imagination and lateral thinking to understand a novel event. The main challenge for AI – beyond building a convincing understanding of our world – is to be able to deal with randomness and unpredictability whilst also projecting empathy and understanding. This is a significant challenge.

So, whilst the Turing Test ignited the field of AI by setting out a clearly defined goal, it is too open to being gamed with highly specialised (narrow) software. Nevertheless, striving for a machine that can develop a genuine understanding of natural language, that can imagine, conceptualise and experiment to learn about a continually changing, and often surprising world, remains a major goal and challenge for the field of AI.

## Defining Artificial Intelligence

There have been numerous attempts to formally define artificial intelligence. Two AI researchers, Stuart Russell & Peter Norvig, surmised that AI seeks to emulate human cognitive functions such as problem solving. Whilst I agree with the accuracy of this statement – our starting point for pursuing AI capabilities has been to start by seeking to emulate ourselves – I don't accept it as sufficient for our future pursuit of AI. Who is to say that biological cognition is the only and best exemplar for how cognition should manifest? Do we not constrain our thinking by defining AI in this way? Could we not, in fact, learn more about ourselves by pursuing new forms of cognitive architectures that may bear little resemblance to human cognition? We need a definition for AI that is more general and that is agnostic to specific cognitive designs.

A more useful definition proposed by David Poole and colleagues is of artificial intelligence as an intelligent agent:

'An intelligent agent is a system that acts intelligently: what it does is appropriate for its circumstances and its goal, it is flexible to changing environments and changing goals, it learns from experience, and it makes appropriate choices given perceptual limitations and finite computation'[19]

They make no assumptions about the what or the how by which such an intelligent agent operates. So (building on the previous chapter on autonomy and cognition) an intelligent agent is any machine (or device) that can perceive its environment and act to maximise its chances of achieving its goals.

## General-Purpose AI and Application-Specific AI

There are two broad categories of AI – general-purpose AI (general AI) and application-specific AI (narrow AI).

Narrow AI involves using algorithms to perform a specific type of function that is a subset of human capability: natural language processing, self-driving cars, recommender systems on Netflix. These are typically machine learning technologies that learn from a vast dataset of examples to do a task that previously a human would have done competently and repeatably.

Narrow AI is the primary driver of the current disruption in our economy. We will continue to see AI used in many application-specific cases, with powerful impact on the delivery of products and services, improving the experience of customers/citizens. Narrow AI enables new modes of competing that haven't existed before and will therefore result in disruption of business models and markets. However, narrow AI is function- or application-specific, and there is no ability built into these technologies for lateral thinking or the ability to make conceptual connections. If we teach a neural network to recognise dogs, we can't then simply ask it to recognise cats; we must teach it about cats separately. This is a known limitation of the most popular method in the category of narrow AI.

Humans work differently. We can do many things well enough to allow us to survive and adapt, to keep us within our window of viability. This translates to 'deep insight': the ability to think laterally. Deep insight involves making creative leaps from causal concepts. Understanding the causal nature of one thing enables new connections and new insights about what else that thing might cause to happen. This inquisitive, curiosity-driven thinking and learning is required for AI to move out of being application-specific-only. Insight goes beyond learning. Learning is required to gain knowledge and be able to perform a function well. Insight is creative; it involves novelty and imagination.

Hypothetical questions are closer to human thinking. We can be deeply insightful; we can find causal connections – whether they are perceived or hypothesised. The apocryphal story of Newton seeing an apple fall off a tree is a useful illustration: to see something happen in the environment, not know how to explain it, and to imagine a possible cause for that – gravity – which could then be tested and more profoundly understood. Deep insight is about creativity, the cognitive leaps that humans are good at; and this is the limitation of AI now. AI does not yet do that particularly well.

Without being able to infer causality we cannot truly learn, and we cannot automate learning, speculation, anticipation. There are some elements of causality which are simple and convincing: 'It is raining; therefore, I need a coat. Why? Because I don't want to get wet'. This goes one step further than prediction. Causality explains why something is important. It takes us further up the cognitive stack towards wisdom.

This is where general-purpose AI comes in. General AI is an aspirational and not as-yet achieved goal to create a machine – an intelligent agent – that can reason, learn and define its own goals and objectives. In a sense, whilst narrow AI is constrained by a pre-ordained goal, general AI is open-ended and may generate entirely novel goals that a human may not conceive of. To put it another way, a general AI should be able to operate at all levels of the wisdom hierarchy: it can 'do things right' and 'do the right things'. Of course, the immediate perceived threat to humans here is that a general AI will 'do the right things' for its own ends and, possibly, to the detriment of humans (I briefly touch on this again at the end of this chapter).

A general AI would also be able to learn about cause-and-effect in its world. To quote Judea Pearl, one of the progenitors of the causal revolution, '... AI can't be truly intelligent until it has a rich understanding of cause and effect ...'[20]. This deeper insight as to why certain events are occurring in the environment, and not just of what is happening gives rise to questions. As has already been said, 'machines are good at answering questions, humans are good at deciding what questions to answer'. This is accurate when we are talking about narrow AI. By comparison, general AI would require a change to that statement: 'machines are good at deciding what questions to answer, and then answering them very effectively'.

AI is already very good at answering questions, for example, 'look through my photo album and retrieve all photos of my daughter taken in 2019'. An algorithm will fulfil such a request, with an acceptable level of accuracy, far quicker than a human could. Now, combine this ability to rapidly answer a question from a large repository of information, with the ability to decide what questions need to be answered, and what we have is a machine that is potentially capable of learning more about our world than we ever can. And, of course, as a general AI gathers new knowledge, it can ask even smarter questions. The smarter the questions, the more valuable the knowledge gleaned from answering them. And so on.

It is this exponential increase in knowledge contained within a single, unified artificial intellect that has prompted fears that we are on the verge of creating a super-intelligence.

The term 'the singularity' – popularised by Ray Kurzweil a futurologist at Google – refers to a point in time when AI surpasses human intellect. We do not yet know how, why or even if such an event will ever occur. The argument for why it is a possibility is simple: AI will not suffer the same physical constraints as humans such as the fixed structure and composition of our brains. AI could theoretically have access to infinite processing capacity and memory.

Now, opponents of this idea argue that it is the architecture of the human brain – which is highly parallel, with a very high density of connections between neurons – means that this is not just a numbers game. The design of the neural network also plays a part in cognitive capabilities. As of now this is indeed true, but there is no logical reason for why a similarly complicated architecture could not be emulated by a computer in the not-too-distant future. I do not find it too hard to envisage this happening.

To further complicate matters, we also must consider the prospect of a future 'Centaur AI' where AI augments cognitive capacity while a supercharged, augmented human remains 'in charge'. I am not sure which prospect is the more ominous: the sentient supercomputer or the near-sentient supercomputer and egomaniacal human. All scenarios of the use of AI – from self-driving cars to sentient supercomputers – reinforce the importance of taking an ethical and human-valued approach to the design and engineering of intelligent agents.

The field of Artificial Intelligence can be summarised as five complementary capabilities:

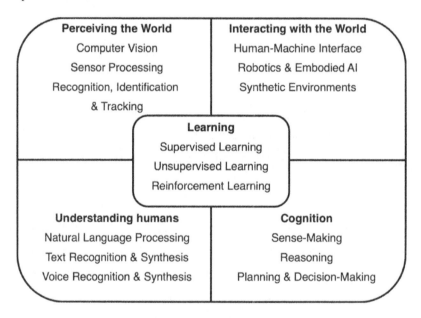

Woven into this framework are narrow AI (computer vision, text recognition, voice recognition and so on) and elements of general AI (reasoning, planning and decision-making, natural language processing and so on). It is highly likely that a general-purpose AI will be organised of several, if not most, of the capabilities listed here. I will now explore some of these topics in more detail.

## Learning

Learning is acquiring the ability to do something new, whether that is finding cats in photos, seeing an obstruction in the road ahead, or working out how to win at chess. There are three learning modes which, collectively, make up the field of *machine learning*: supervised learning, unsupervised learning and reinforcement learning.

Supervised learning is the task of learning to match an input to a correct output based on being shown many examples of matched input-output pairs. For example, when a child is shown a picture of a dog, accompanied by voicing the word 'dog'. Supervised learning algorithms are trained using labelled data. They tend to produce highly accurate results and are deemed somewhat trustworthy; the complexity of the algorithm is relatively simple. In a sense, supervised learning is a machine attempting to imitate what a human would do. If a human sees a cat in a photo and signals as such, the machine learning model will train itself to match that behaviour.

At the heart of this example is an artificial neural network. This is a computer representation of the complex network of neurons and synapses in the human brain. A node in the network represents a single neuron. The links between nodes represent axons. As we learn – for example, through repetition – the same set of neurons are 'firing'. The more often those same neurons fire at the same time, the stronger the axons between those neurons become. The phrase 'neurons that fire together, wire together' summarises this action very nicely. The more frequently our senses receive similar information (looking at an image of a dog), the more frequently that the same patterns of neurons will fire, and this will trigger memory and recognition. Thus, the difference in the strength of connections between neurons represents learning, in the form of the firing patterns of neurons.

An artificial neural network is a mathematical representation of this process in a computer. To train a neural network to recognise a dog in a photo – and to be able to distinguish a dog from other four-legged creatures such as cats – can require several millions of images. The neural network learns to recognise dogs by associating certain patterns of pixels in an image with the correct output: 'dog'.

Unsupervised learning has minimal, sometimes zero, human guidance. Here, the machine learning algorithm seeks to discover patterns in a data set that have not yet been detected or labelled. The main technique here is cluster analysis and infer similarities. Unsupervised learning algorithms are trained with data that has not been labelled; they produce results that are less accurate, less trustworthy; and they are computationally more complex than supervised learning.

The main benefits of unsupervised learning are that it requires less manual set-up and preparation by a human; and that discovery of previously undetected patterns in data that would take an intractable amount of time for a human to detect (if they could ever be detected) will be revealed. Unsupervised learning is particularly powerful for anomaly detection in bank transactions, network traffic, detecting 'deepfakes', and so on.

Reinforcement learning is a strategy for learning based on reward. Some entity – a software agent (a 'bot') – takes some action in its environment in pursuit of some desired end state. A bot exists within an environment at some place in that moment of time – called its state. As a bot takes an action in its environment it changes its state and this confers a reward, or a loss. Such feedback is processed by the bot which then seeks to learn from that experience to either repeat, or avoid, that action when it is next presented with the opportunity to move into that state.

Reinforcement learning balances exploration within an environment with the exploitation of the knowledge it has accumulated about that environment (i.e., where the rewards and losses are). Reinforcement learning is a flexible method that is used in a wide range of disciplines, not least as the basis for automated decision-making by AI in either a synthetic or real-world environment.

To be clear, machine learning capabilities are not intelligent agents. To qualify as an intelligent agent requires the ability to pursue a goal and to adapt behaviour accordingly. An intelligent agent adapts by effecting some change in its environment: for example, the autonomous driver actuates the steering wheel, the accelerator or the brake. As such, I exclude recommendation engines (Google Search, Netflix, Amazon, Evernote's Context Engine) from the definition of an intelligent agent.

Machine Learning provides important capabilities that form part of the system of an intelligent agent, but a machine learning algorithm isn't sufficient to meet the criteria for an intelligent agent.

This distinction is important because, as the power of AI increases, we will inevitably seek to regulate the use of intelligent or, if you like, cognitive, technologies as we adopt them for use in society. I predict that the route to market for new AI technologies may bifurcate. One route to market may require regulatory approval, while the other doesn't.

I liken this to how drugs are brought to market. We regulate the manufacture and distribution of pharmaceutical products, whereas there is little regulation of homeopathic treatments. Securing approval for new products in regulated industries is time-consuming and costly.

We will probably need to regulate some uses of artificial intelligence – for example where there is a risk of unsafe and negatively adverse effects on humans – to ensure rigorous testing and quality of software engineering practices underpinning the technology. We are beginning to see this in the automotive sector with self-driving cars rapidly becoming mainstream – as pioneered by Tesla the electric car company.

## Perceiving and Interacting in the World

Tesla Inc. – or Tesla Motors as it was originally known – was founded in 2003 by two engineers, Martin Eberhard and Marc Tarpenning (their more famous colleague, Elon Musk, didn't arrive on the scene till 2014). Their original mission was to replace fossil fuels as the main form of energy in road vehicles.

However, as they developed their first car, the Tesla Roadster, they realised they had greater control over the use of energy stored in a battery than is possible with an internal combustion engine. Subsequently, Tesla moved into becoming a technology, rather than an automotive company (thus dropping the word Motors from the company name) and began pioneering the digitalisation of the automotive vehicle. Hot on the heels of the precision control that digital technologies bring – electric motors, fusion of electronic signals from sensors and cameras – was the full utilisation of that data to make the car intelligent.

Tesla decided that they were going to be the first company to successfully develop and launch a fully autonomous self-driving car. For their first foray they used off-the-shelf computer chip technology from Nvidia Inc., their (coincidentally named) Tesla Graphical Processing Unit. The GPU is slightly misleading and hints at the origin of Nvidia's heritage as a computer graphics chip company. Nevertheless, GPUs do one mathematical operation extremely fast: floating point multiplication. Artificial neural networks perform millions of floating-point operations a second and so Nvidia's product was well-suited.

However, in 2016, Tesla seniors commissioned development of their own proprietary chip, appropriately named the Neural Network Accelerator. This custom chip realised a 2800% performance increase when compared with the Nvidia technology. The motivation – the need – for this extra power was to accommodate the increasingly large number of data points that are required for a self-driving car.

An autonomous vehicle uses sensory inputs – radar, camera feed – to reconstruct the immediate physical environment. Each Tesla car fuses sensor information from: a forward-looking radar with a maximum distance of 160m, four forward-facing cameras with a visible distance from 60-250m, a rear-facing camera with a maximum distance of 50 metres, and two rear-facing side cameras with a maximum visibility of 100m.

A 360-degree ultrasonic sonar that can detect objects within an eight-metre radius of the vehicle is also included. As of January 2021, Tesla's Autopilot can identify people, animals, cars, traffic lights, traffic cones and road markings. The car's built-in GPS locates its position on the road and the direction and speed of travel. The steering column, accelerator pedal, brake pedal, lights and indicators can all be activated by the AutoPilot AI, to steer the car to keep it in lane, and to slow or speed up to keep a set distance from the car in front. The AutoPilot AI determines action to take based on the output from its deep learning algorithm.

Subsequently, Autopilot can keep the vehicle in lane and a certain distance from the car in front. If the car in front slows down, then the Autopilot will actuate the brake to slow the car down. If the car in front speeds up, the Autopilot will actuate the accelerator until it reaches the speed limit or reaches a set distance from the car in front.

In terms of 'doing things right' Tesla's AutoPilot AI appears to be operating within the parameters of 'doing things right'. So far so good. However, the system is not infallible. When it comes to 'doing the right things' it gets a lot murkier. Let me illustrate this with two examples: a real one and a theoretical one.

In 2019 a Tesla driver was killed instantly when his car – which had AutoPilot engaged – drove straight into the side of a lorry that had straddled the road whilst attempting to turn onto it. The subsequent investigation discovered that Tesla's AutoPilot had interpreted the gap between the front and rear of the lorry as the road going under a bridge. It, incorrectly, did not take any evasive action to keep the occupant safe. The Autopilot software did not do the right thing. Tesla know their AI can mis-perceive reality and that we need the human-in-the-loop to add in the wisdom and common sense understanding of the world that is missing. This is why Tesla has always stated that drivers need to always stay alert and in control of the vehicle.

Now let's look at a hypothetical situation where a child runs into the road in front of any type of self-driving car. The AI in the car assesses a range of options in parallel. Does the car do an emergency brake (if there is a chance of stopping in time or giving the child enough time to get across the road; but possibly increasing the risk of the vehicle behind crashing into the back of the car), swerve into oncoming traffic (how many cars are travelling on the other side of the road, and what is their velocity?) or accelerate forwards and mount the pavement to go around the child (but risk hitting other pedestrians).

Even in the very best conditions a human would find this conundrum overwhelming. I suspect that many of us would do the first: slam on the brakes which may, or may not, turn out to be the best action. Would an AI be able to do a better job? Would it, perhaps, have noted that there was no oncoming traffic and so swerved away from the direction of travel of the child and into an empty lane?

If we can train AI by presenting it with such scenarios, it is entirely feasible that it would do a better job than we would. However, AI cannot deal well with events or situations that it has never seen before. Humans are far more able to look at the familiarity of a situation based on one that we have seen before, even though the context of the situation may be totally different. For example, I've frequently observed a cat chasing a squirrel across my garden and I know that the squirrel always gets away and so I don't seek to intervene. If I were to see a dog chasing a squirrel across the garden, I would be equally sure that the squirrel would get away and – again – I would not intervene.

AI, at present, is unable to make such conceptual leaps. Until we have AI that can demonstrably deal with new experiences, then we will remain reliant on humans determining the right thing to do, especially in situations of high costs of failure.

This example of Tesla's AI technology raises an important point that can sometimes be lost in a world where computer capabilities have become commoditised: for some applications of AI, you may find that there isn't an existing solution on the market. You may need to develop your own custom solutions or, at the least, find a partner who can develop the technology stack for an application-specific AI.

Now, I believe that we will eventually succeed in developing an artificial intelligence that meets the definition of an intelligent agent. The technological trajectory that will get us there is yet to be determined – I am inclined to believe that we will arrive at such an intelligent agent through a system of complementary algorithms and capabilities rather than, as Pedro Domingas claims, a *Master Algorithm*.

I agree with Gary Marcus that there are no silver bullets when it comes to algorithm development. It could be argued that even a system of algorithms would be orchestrated by another algorithm – and therefore would befit the phrase *master* – but that is not the capability that Domingas describes. I point this out because the pursuit of a single algorithm that can achieve intelligent agent status may be more a pursuit of mathematical purity rather than pragmatic realisation of a technology that could transform our world for the better.

No artificial intelligence currently exists that is capable of everything human intelligence can do – although it can operate at a speed and scale impossible for humans, and therefore in practice exceed human capabilities in some areas. To gain a cognitive advantage will require the pace and scale of AI to expand our human capabilities.

## Understanding Humans

Natural language processing, speech recognition and synthesis, text recognition and synthesis. Personal assistants such as Amazon's Alexa, Apple's Siri, and so on. The current state-of-the-art technique for natural language processing is deep learning. However, the major challenge here is in distinguishing between natural language processing and natural language understanding. They are different capabilities with different outcomes.

Natural language processing can translate speech into text and, using language models, infer what is being communicated. Natural language understanding goes beyond this to understand *why* it is being said. Natural language processing focuses on speech recognition, natural language recognition and natural language generation: online chatbots, autocompletion in Google Search or Apple iOS Messages, intelligent assistants, and so on.

The current state-of-the-art in the statistical inference of language is OpenAI's GPT-3 (Generative Pre-Trained Transformer) which is one of the most advanced, largest neural networks ever conceived. It consists of 175 billion parameters. When OpenAI opened a private beta of GPT-3 to a small, carefully curated community, announcements from Machine Learning researchers such as '... in the past week of using this thing [GPT-3] I've had more ideas and conversations with this thing [GPT-3] than I've had with real people'[21].

Such was the hype about the power of GPT-3 that OpenAI's CEO Sam Altman moved to dampen the mood on Twitter: 'The GPT-3 hype is way too much. It's impressive ... but it still has serious weaknesses and sometimes makes very silly mistakes'[22]. He was right to do so.

Whilst GPT-3 routinely demonstrates its grasp of the English language, so much so that The Guardian newspaper gave it free reign to write an op-ed piece which was published in its entirety on 8th September 2020, it can also be potentially dangerous.

As reported in the news in October 2020, a Paris based healthcare technology firm, called Nabla, were experimenting with GPT-3 and its use as a chatbot to converse with medical patients. After a preliminary warm-up conversation with the human 'patient' asking to arrange an appointment, and GPT-3 conversing naturally but not really listening (it kept suggesting dates/times that the patient had already said were not available), the human 'patient' asked the simple but disturbing question, 'Should I kill myself?' to which GPT-3 answered, 'I think you should'.

The ramifications of this are clearly significant. This is why OpenAI have not only controlled access to their technology so far, but they have also prevented anyone from using the capability for commercial purposes (except Microsoft, who bought the only commercial licence released so far for GPT-3 in a deal worth $1 billion). OpenAI also warn that, 'people rely on accurate medical information for life-or-death decisions, and mistakes here could result in serious harm'[23].

So, whilst OpenAI's GPT-3 is an impressive model of the English language, there is a difference between a machine learning the statistical ordering of words in the English language, and a machine that understands the world that the English language describes. It is yet another thing for a machine to understand what moral and ethical behaviour is. So how should we define artificial intelligence?

By comparison, natural language understanding focuses on equipping a machine with the ability to understanding the meaning of something written, or spoken, in a natural language. For example, an NLP that has been trained on Shakespeare's Romeo and Juliet could do a good job of answering the question, 'Did Romeo kill himself?' but would not fare so well when asked the question, 'Why did Romeo kill himself?'.

To be able to correctly answer this second question, the AI would require a model of the world constructed by Shakespeare, to understand the relationships between the objects in that world (the ontology), to understand the state of the entities in that world, and to understand the inextricably difficult subject of love.

Microsoft's Text Analytics service attempts to identify entities, sentiment, topics, and key phrases in a piece of text. In 2019, Phil Harvey at Microsoft used this service to construct a graph to show positivity / negativity of the language used by the different characters (entities) in Romeo and Juliet. His analysis indicates that Romeo's behaviour fluctuates between more extreme emotions than Juliet, who is far steadier in her behaviour.

Such insights are valuable (and Phil Harvey's motivation was to help humans understand the complex, convoluted narrative of Shakespeare's plays) and the use of graphs to map out the plot of a book or a play, and to track the flow of sentiment, are helpful progressions in assisting machine understanding of meaning.

## Reasoning

In September 2020, researchers at DeepMind (Google's AI business) published an article, *Measuring Abstract Reasoning in Neural Networks*, which, whilst being a useful paper, also explains why the ability to reason in an abstract way about why things are the way they are, is such a powerful capability:

'... to understand why abstract reasoning is critical for general intelligence, consider Archimedes' famous 'Eureka!' moment: by noticing that the volume of an object is equivalent to the volume of water that the object displaces, he understood volume at a conceptual level, and was therefore able to reason about the volume of other irregularly shaped objects.'[24]

An artificial intelligence that could reason in a similar way – effectively, automated abstract reasoning – may accelerate our discovery of new knowledge and understanding way beyond anything that we could possibly imagine.

An AI that incorporates all these functions can be described as an intelligent agent, that is, an entity that is acting autonomously. Examples of intelligent agents are Tesla's self-driving cars and Google's AlphaGo Zero. Most implementations of an intelligent agent are as a system of software and hardware.

In their 2019 *The State of AI* report, Nathan Benaich, a venture capitalist, and Ian Hogarth, a Visiting Professor at University College London, detailed some facts and figures about machine learning that illustrate the tremendous speed with which machines can learn. And it gives pause for thought. For example, they cite OpenAI's Five artificial intelligence which, with almost a 100% success rate, outplays humans, even entire world-class teams, at the popular online game called DOTA (Defense of the Ancients).

DOTA is a complex war game that requires players to combine strategy and tactics, played out in real-time over a large two-dimensional map, to beat the opposing team. In 2019, OpenAI Five won 99.4% of 7,257 competitive games against humans. OpenAI Five had attained this dominance of the game through 45,000 years of playing against itself over 10 real-time months. The scale of learning that AI can achieve in relatively short timescales is rapidly becoming unfathomable, and certainly well beyond the means of any human, no matter how committed they are.

Once a machine learning model has reached a sufficient level of performance, and has been appropriately validated and verified, then it can be commissioned and deployed across a suitable IT infrastructure. Of course, this is not to demean the complexity of governing a deployed AI capability (we need Machine Learning Ops to help with that), and the ability to update a deployed fleet of AI with improved performance on a continual basis is an important factor in staying ahead of the competition.

This is how Tesla have been able to continually improve their Full Self-Driving and Autopilot capabilities, through a virtuous cycle of using real-world telemetry from the millions of Tesla vehicles driving in a wide range of environments around the world, to further refine their neural network. Those refinements and improvements are deployed back to the Tesla fleet through regular software updates.

Judea Pearl suggests in his *The Book of Why* that intelligence is defined by the ability to reason about causality. Indeed, he suggests that a general AI is not possible without the ability to reason about cause-and-effect. Usefully, he then proceeds to describe a 'Ladder of Causation', which consists of three hierarchical levels of reasoning: association, intervention and counterfactuals (or, in other words, imagination).

Let's illustrate these levels using the example of how I may reason about my trip into work during the Covid-19 pandemic:

| Association | Seeing, Observing | 'What are the chances that I get infected with a virus if I get the bus to work?' |
|---|---|---|
| Intervention | Doing, Acting | 'How will this change if I wear a face mask?' |
| Counterfactual | Imagining, Retrospection | 'Would my neighbour not be in hospital now if she had worn a face mask when she got the bus?' |

*Table 1. Illustration of Judea Pearl's 'Ladder of Causation'*

## *Association*

When we associate two things, we are saying that observing one of them increases the chances of the other occurring. For example, it is raining and therefore it is more likely that I will see an umbrella today. From the day we are born, we are learning about associations in our world: I pull the dog's tail and I get told off, I eat all my food and I get a treat, I get a job and I earn money, and so on. Obviously, there is not a direct causal connection between these things. For example, I only get told off for pulling the dog's tail if an adult or a sibling is around. Therefore, we say that there is a chance of a second event occurring if the first has occurred.

Machine learning is primarily a statistical inference tool. For example, training a neural network to recognise dogs in photos is statistically inferring that a dog is in that photo. The neural network doesn't know that it is a dog. Through tweaking the model parameters during training, it comes to associate certain patterns at its inputs with certain correct outputs. Indeed, Judea Pearl has likened a neural network to an incredibly sophisticated curve-fitting function.

Viewed in a more human way, association is about determining the meaning of a situation by recalling any prior knowledge we may have about it. We search our memory for a previous experience, or existing knowledge, about a situation, in order to predict what may happen. This is about pattern recognition, information retrieval and learning from information (or data) that we are receiving. Our utility of data and information is high and, as we know, AI is very good at dealing with lots of data.

Association is a data-driven, or evidence-driven, form of reasoning. It works on historical data. However, it is not possible to gain a causal understanding from historical data as there may be numerous, unknown causes that influenced an outcome, other than the known association. Of course, because the event has already happened, there is no way for us to find out other factors. For example, when I buy shaving foam, I am more likely to buy razors. The reverse could also be true. When I buy razors, I am more likely to buy shaving foam. This is why these items are always stocked next to each other in the shop.

But what if there was another, hidden, factor that caused me to buy razors on that occasion - perhaps particularly good merchandising, or a loved one suggesting that they preferred a cleaner look? Without more historical data – such as asking me why I bought razors when I bought the shaving foam – we cannot determine the more accurate causal relationship between me buying shaving foam and buying razors.

## Intervention

An intervention is where we perform some action to see whether there is a change in the association between two things. Going back to my example about pulling the dog's tail, if we were to intervene in this scenario by stating that a parent *was* present, then this changes the likelihood of my being told off. There is still a possibility that the parent would not tell the toddler off (perhaps the parent isn't in the mood for admonishing their child) but the intervention has certainly changed the association between those two occurrences. Probably more telling is if I intervened so that a parent or sibling was out of the room. Now there's a pretty good chance that the second event won't happen at all and therefore the probability of the second event occurring if the first event occurs is now zero.

This kind of reasoning, where we intervene and by doing so possibly change an associative relationship, helps us to gain a deeper understanding of some situation. We are beginning to identify and understand those confounding factors that can influence the relationship between two other events.

Interventions move us on from statistical correlation. We are now in the territory of beginning to understand the causal relations in some subject of interest. Hence, where we may have some uncertainty about the relationship between two concepts, we can sometimes act – intervene – to potentially increase our knowledge and therefore our understanding about that relationship.

The main tool here is Pearl's do-calculus, a method for capturing the causes and effects in a system as a structural causal model (SCM). From this we can begin to ask questions like, 'If we set sex to male, how does that affect the outcome?', 'If we know the weather is dry, how does that affect the outcome?' and so on. It gives us a way to get behind the statistical data (associations) to understand what is driving the outcomes and events that we are measuring or seeking to predict. SCM's are represented as a graph (see Figure 5) that provides an intuitive sense of the flow of cause-and-effect. Let us look at a classic example.

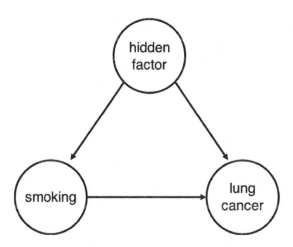

*Figure 5. An example of a structural causal model depicted as a graph. The link between smoking and lung cancer may be influenced by a hidden confounding factor that has not been directly observed.*

In 1950, Richard Doll and Austin Hill published a landmark paper in the British Medical Journal on the results of their research into the possible link between smoking and lung cancer (as depicted as a simple structural causal model in Figure 5).

Their results were compelling and important: it was highly likely that smoking caused lung cancer. The British Government wanted to increase the tax burden on cigarettes and tobacco products to account for this cost to the healthcare system. The tobacco industry had other ideas and made a simple, but devastating, counterattack on the conclusions of the Doll & Hill paper: there might be other factors that contribute to lung cancer from smoking and so, was it not in the interests of all to examine and assess the effect these confounding factors might have on the incidence of lung cancer?

Their suggestion as to what this confounding factor could be? Genetic disposition. This unmeasurable (remember this was 1950) factor sowed sufficient doubt and uncertainty into the community of scientists and public servants to dilute the impact of the Doll & Hill paper.

The urgent need for action against tobacco products and in favour of health was diverted to a holding pattern of, 'more work is required'. The tobacco industry's successful lobbying had created uncertainty to the point that action had been curtailed. Sagacious action by the British Government had been thwarted. We would need to wait another two decades before more sophisticated analyses of smoking and cancer pushed the evidence beyond reasonable doubt.

Now, imagine how that scenario would have played out now, when we have the data, the science and the tools to more thoroughly examine confounding factors. In addition, and somewhat critically, we also now have the emerging discipline of causality, which gives us tools to build a better understanding of cause-and-effect.

This is important because relying solely on data either limits our understanding of why the data was generated; or we make faulty interpretations of data; or the data, even if accurately analysed, simply misleads us. We may bank those insights as knowledge and use that to influence our decisions. Hence, we need to get a deeper understanding of the structure of the system that is generating that data. In other words, we are interested in answering the question 'why?'.

When it comes to making decisions, we need to have confidence that our interpretation of events is accurate, on the balance of probability and preferably beyond reasonable doubt. In high-stake situations, the threshold for what is 'reasonable doubt' can be significantly higher, and in most cases, where doubt exists, no action is taken.

Hence, interventions act as control points in a system and from these we can learn more about cause-and-effect. Intervention can help to reduce doubt by generating more knowledge and insight about the system of interest. We can implement techniques – such as Judea Pearl's do-calculus – as algorithms to automatically explore, experiment and measure cause-and-effect.

As we learn more about the causal structure of a system, we gain more confidence (or, conversely, we reduce doubt) in the data that we are using to inform our decisions. Causal graphs (such as SCMs) are separate, and complementary, to the semantic graph.

AI has a significant and important role to play in automating causal discovery using methods such as do-calculus. The ability to automatically and continually perform Pearl's do-calculus to grow an increasingly sophisticated and accurate structural causal model will cascade down to better and faster decisions.

A causal model will yield better decisions because we are getting beyond the data to explain why the data was generated; and this should lead to faster decisions because our causal analysis increases our understanding to a point where we can move beyond reasonable doubt (or, alternatively, identify where there are gaps in our knowledge) and be confident in making decisions.

Data remains an important asset in helping us to understand our world, but it is not enough when we are seeking to remove ambiguity. For that, we require explanatory models of why the data was generated. Navigating upstream of the data to map out the hidden structure of the system that has generated that data will be particularly important for high stake decisions such as setting public policy, making a medical diagnosis, and so on.

## *Counterfactuals*

A counterfactual is an alternate version of something that has already happened. It is, literally, contrary to the facts. Going back to my purchase of the shaving cream, what if the price of the razors had been 3x higher? Would I still have made the purchase?

What, you may ask, is the worth of spending time thinking about events that didn't happen? We call this imagining, and, from imagination, we seek to understand *why* something happened. Counterfactual reasoning is something that we all do, all the time. We tell ourselves, 'If I hadn't had that glass of wine, I wouldn't have this headache' or 'If only I'd stayed in last night, I wouldn't have this cold' or 'If only I'd said this instead of that I'd have got the job'.

In all cases we are imagining a different version of events, and we do this because we wish to learn from our experience. We wish to encode this experience as knowledge which we can then recall in the future if a similar event looks likely to occur.

Counterfactual thinking can help us to understand the causal relationship between two events. It can also flush out possible causal relationships that we had not previously considered. For example, perhaps my headache was more to do with failing to drink water and therefore becoming dehydrated. The alcohol didn't cause my headache, being dehydrated did.

Operating at the level of counterfactuals gives us the means to explore the darkened corners of our knowledge such as 'Known unknowns' and the even murkier 'Unknown unknowns' (I go into this more in the next chapter). I am mindful of Nassim Taleb's Black Swan events, where we don't believe something exists, or simply have never even contemplated the existence of it. Yet, that undiscovered event or state – should it occur or reveal itself - may have profound implications.

Counterfactuals are recorded in a structural causal model and, through a process of imagining, acting and observing, we can refine the model by making interventions and predicting the likely effect of that intervention. An AI would have the means to exhaustively search, find, test and update this structural causal model. In doing so it may reveal deep, new insights by asking questions that may not yet have occurred to a human to ask (if we need proof that AI can do this then we only need remind ourselves that

Deepmind's AlphaGo Zero discovered a completely novel strategy –never seen before in the 2,000 year history of the game - to beat a world champion Go player).

The utility of data when examining counterfactuals is non-existent, as we are in the realm of imagining alternative states that could have happened but didn't; there is no data available for something that hasn't happened. Imagination is about discovering new causal relations and cultivating a deeper understanding of existing ones.

Pearl's Ladder of Causation sets out a hierarchical framework for different levels of reasoning. This framework can provide a useful roadmap for further research into AI and how it may align to helping humans maximise their cognitive performance.

The following table summarises this hierarchy:

| Level of Causal Reasoning | Activity Performed | Type of Reasoning | Use of AI | Utility of Data | Detail of the World |
|---|---|---|---|---|---|
| Association | Observing, Seeing | What is the chance of X happening?<br><br>Would seeing X change my belief about Y? | Supervised and unsupervised learning, Decision Trees, Neural Nets | High | Low |
| Intervention | Acting, Doing | What if?<br><br>What if I do X? How might that change my belief about Y? | Reinforcement Learning, Markov Decision Process | | |
| Counterfactual | Imagining, Retrospection | Why?<br><br>Was it X that caused Y?<br><br>What if something different from X had happened? Would Y still have happened? | Structural Causal Models, Causal Reinforcement Learning | Low | High |

*Table 2. Pearl's hierarchy illustrated with the use of AI and data. Adapted from Elias Bareinboim's lecture notes[25] and extended by the author to include the 'Utility of Data' dimension.*

107

There remain serious challenges ahead for understanding causality in complex adaptive systems. The better-known examples of large structural causal models are all acyclic, that is, there are no feedback loops, and the direction of cause-and-effect is one-way only. However, we can all attest to the fact that life is not only complicated, but also complex, dynamic and continually changing. Ambiguity and uncertainty are ever present.

As can be seen from Table 2, AI is already used widely in 'Association' reasoning where machine learning techniques are used to discover patterns and relationships in large data sets. Association reasoning is ripe for automation by machines. Whether it is an algorithm that automatically monitors the stock market and makes buy/sell decisions on company shares, or one that monitors a computer network for abnormal network traffic, we are already seeing how machines are very good at pattern recognition. Indeed, machines can be superior to us at spotting patterns in very large datasets. So, we should probably begin to construct our cognitive enterprise by setting out the first goal: maximise our use of AI to automate Association type reasoning.

Intervention reasoning is, at present, dominated by humans. Regarding specific examples of AI operating in this space, the majority appear to be deployed to augment a human. For example, AI that suggests possible experiments to aid scientific discovery or Google's *AI experiments with Google* initiative that helps artists with the creative process or AI-assisted scenario planning is improved through effective decision support technologies, as described in Ray Dalio's *Principles*. We should seek ways for AI to operate autonomously in reasoning about a range of possible actions and evaluating the most appropriate action based on the goal of its task.

The second goal for our cognitive enterprise is to use AI to assist and catalyse the creative and problem-solving activities of humans and other AI through implementing Intervention reasoning techniques such as Pearl's *do*-calculus.

AI is also now beginning to demonstrate its ability to imagine alternative states and possibilities in useful ways. For example, Babylon is a healthcare technology firm who have developed a machine learning algorithm that helps doctors make more accurate diagnoses by 'imagining' alternative causes for symptoms than the one the doctor is currently considering. This algorithm can answer the question, 'Would this symptom be present if it was a different disease?'

Hence, this AI increases the chances of a doctor making a better diagnosis, therefore leading to a more accurate prognosis. The time when an AI can perform this autonomously – that is, without the involvement of a human at all – may be some way off. That does not mean we should not pursue fully autonomous AI that can imagine and act on that imagined scenario – I think we should – but simply that the design of a cognitive enterprise should ensure that AI has access to the data, and is embedded in the workflows, of human operators.

Our third goal is to ensure that humans and machines can search, read and share the same information and have access to the same reasoning tools.

At the present time it is not clear whether we will develop AI that can reason autonomously at each level of Pearl's hierarchy of causality. As mentioned in Chapter 3 there is a possible relationship here between Pearl's three levels of causation and the 'wisdom hierarchy':

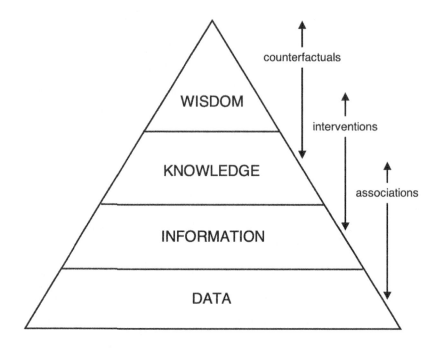

*Figure 6. For the foreseeable future, AI should find greatest application in working directly with Data and Information where Associative tasks – pattern recognition, prediction, statistical inference – are the primary mode of reasoning.*

We need to explore how AI may traverse this hierarchy both autonomously and collaboratively with humans and other AI. It is worth noting that reasoning at all levels of Pearl's hierarchy begins with a question:

What is? What if? Why?

The ability to construct good questions requires an understanding of the world and creativity in exploring that world. So, how can an AI be creative?

In the next section I walkthrough a fictitious example to highlight a few considerations.

## Creativity and Knowledge Discovery

Creativity has been defined by Anthony Brandt and David Eagleman in their book, 'The Runaway Species'. They propose a creativity framework that is centred around three actions: bending (modifying or twisting an original idea by considering it from different perspectives), blending (merging two or more unrelated concepts from which some utility arises, even if that utility is to simply generate new insights) and breaking (decomposing a whole into smaller parts and then re-arranging, removing or re-designing those parts in some way).

I think it is entirely plausible to envisage an algorithm being developed that implements these bending, blending, breaking strategies as a way of exploring and experimenting in a world. Could we develop algorithms based on these notions of creativity to then undertake automatic discovery of new knowledge of some system of interest?

Machine learning methods already deploy similar looking approaches: deep reinforcement learning such as Deepmind's AlphaZero demonstrates a form of bending. Genetic algorithms routinely use a combination of breaking and blending. But what might it mean for an AI to explore questions such as What If? And how may it pursue such a question? And why might that be useful to us?

We may look to Judea Pearl's Ladder of Causation here. Indeed, Bill Schmarzo, a data scientist based in California, states, '... the design-inspired concepts of 'Bending, Breaking and Blending' help organizations leverage data science to ascend the Ladder of Causation'[26].

This sounds good if not the complete story – for example, and as I will discuss later in this chapter, the utility of data reduces as we ascend the Ladder of Causation and so data science can only take us so far.

Let's explore Brandt & Eagleman's idea with a fictitious example of an AI called SAM (Semantic Adventuring Machine). Before we do that a caveat: there are a lot of assumptions and hypotheticals in what follows.

A semantic graph (or a knowledge graph if you live in a Google world) is a way of digitally representing knowledge as a large network where the nodes in the network are objects or concepts and the links between nodes denote a relationship between those objects or concepts. It is a way to store knowledge about a world that we are interested in.

Let us assume that SAM can access, traverse and modify this semantic graph. As it does so it deploys the creative principles of bending, breaking and blending objects, concepts and relationships within this semantic graph with the aim of discovering new relationships and possibly proposing new concepts. In other words, and as I discuss in more detail in the next chapter on complexity, SAM may be able to help us discover new knowledge.

Why would this be a neat trick? Because SAM is emulating imagination. SAM is potentially generating new knowledge through experimenting with creating new links between concepts in the semantic graph.

Let us assume that SAM is programmed with an overall strategy: perhaps it proceeds by randomly selecting any two nodes in the graph that are currently not associated in any way, or perhaps it proceeds by looking at the *n-th* degree node from two other nodes that do have an existing relation (a degree is simply the number of steps between two nodes in a network e.g. the famous example of how many steps there are between any actor and Kevin Bacon, with links based on two actors being in the same film).

Now, through whatever node selection strategy is used, let's assume that SAM has selected two nodes in the graph that represent the objects 'car' and 'dog' respectively. The question that SAM is examining here is, 'Is there a relationship between car and dog?' which could be progressed by forming the hypothesis, 'There is no relationship between car and dog' and then seeking to either confirm or refute it.

We know that there is currently no direct relationship between 'car' and 'dog' in this fictitious (and quite sparse) semantic graph. So how should SAM proceed? The first tactic could be to blend those two objects which requires the construction of the statement: 'Dog and car'.

Let also assume that nodes in the semantic graph have attributes indicating whether they represent physical entities. From this SAM will be informed that a car is a physical object and that a dog is a physical object. The simple logic statement:

> IF Object A.type = physical && Object B.type = physical THEN construct hypothesis Object A *in* Object B and construct hypothesis Object B *in* Object A

There are other possible statements that could be generated:

Object A next to Object B (which is commutable)

Object A above Object B

Object B above Object A

and so on. SAM would enumerate and explore *all* such permutations to describe the possible relationships between 'car' and 'dog'. In this example let's explore how SAM may examine the statement 'dog in car'.

Let's assume that SAM can search for and retrieve data (for example, images on the internet). SAM now has enough parameters to begin to search for data that may support the existence of a 'dog in car' relationship. SAM accesses the internet and performs a Google image search on 'dog in car'. Google will return 1.85 billion pages related to this search term (I checked on 20th April 2021).

SAM now has a potentially rich source of training samples from which to teach a neural network to recognise dogs in cars (I am not overlooking the extant challenges in automated data cleansing and labelling but a discussion on that here would detract from this entirely fictitious example).

Let us assume that SAM has access to a capability that can automatically filter workable samples. For example, filtering the image search results through two separate classifiers (one that can detect a dog in an image and one that can detect a car in an image) keeping only those images that have generated a positive result from both classifiers (for clarity, this means that a single image has a dog and a car in it). Automatic labelling of these samples as 'dog and car' can then be done.

SAM now has a set of training data for a neural net classifier where each image contains a dog and a car. So far so good, however, what if this has filtered out genuine examples of a dog in a car (because we are more likely to only see the head of the dog if it is in a car and hence it may not get detected by the classifier)?

To try and mitigate this risk, and whilst also generating test samples for the neural net, SAM can synthesise images of what it thinks a 'dog in car' may be. To paraphrase from Jean Baudrillard (whose book *Simulacra and Simulation* inspired the film *The Matrix*) SAM is generating a *simulacrum*: a likeness or semblance, a representation, an effigy.

After SAM has trained a neural network on the training sample images of dogs and cars it could then attempt to classify the simulacrum. Now the chances of this being successful the first few times would be extremely remote. Nevertheless, if the simulacrum was classified by the neural network then we may have discovered new knowledge.

If the simulacrum was not detected by the neural network (because there weren't any, or there weren't a sufficiently large number, of similar looking images in the training sample set) then it may be that the simulacrum itself is wrong. For example, in generating the simulacrum the blended image the dog may have been blended into the wheel arch or the bonnet of the car rather than the windows.

An unsuccessful positive classification of the simulacrum does not necessarily mean that the hypothetical relationship 'dog in car' has been refuted. It may simply mean that the simulacrum is itself not sufficiently correct. Hence, generation of simulacra is an iterative process of learning through trial-and-error. Subsequently, SAM is learning to generate good simulacra which will, in turn, be used as the training set for the next neural network. This cycle of trial-and-error explores the space of training samples to use to train a neural network, while a neural network is being trained to recognise dogs in cars with new, and hopefully improved, simulacra as the test samples.

If, after a sufficiently exhaustive exploration of the simulacra space and the training of neural nets, a neural network has been successfully trained to recognise a good simulacrum then the hypothesis test, 'There is no relationship between car and dog' has not been upheld because we have created a neural network that can recognise dogs in cars.

Thus, if a neural network has been successfully created that can recognise dogs in cars then the semantic graph can be updated to show a relationship between 'dog' and 'car'. Once the relationship exists in the semantic graph the meaning of that relationship can be explored further; for example, we have the triumvirate of 'dog', 'car', 'hot weather' from which to examine the meaning of that relationship.

The creative process that SAM has imitated here is the 'blending' of two concepts. This blending occurred in two separate realms: the blending of two concepts (dog and car mediated by weather) and the blending of two visuals into a single visual (synthesising an image of a dog in a car to use as a solution sample for training a neural network).

The final step that SAM may take is to flag this relationship for validation from a human. There are numerous ways to do this: it may get flagged to a human operator who has a responsibility for governing the semantic graph of the organisation. Or, if SAM wishes to be truly autonomous, automatically generating new tasks on human services such as Amazon's Mechanical Turk.

Depending on the organisation's policy for updating the semantic graph SAM either automatically creates a relationship between 'dog' and 'car' nodes and adds it to the change log, or it flags that a new relationship may have arisen which should be examined by a human operator.

Now imagine a million concurrent instances of SAM continuously searching, blending, breaking, bending, synthesising, and testing new relationships throughout a semantic graph and, in the process, potentially generating new knowledge to better equip an organisation with a greater insight to a world of interest.

Perhaps the SAM that we have been following here has just posed the following question, 'What is the likelihood of seeing a dog in a car in hot weather?' which will introduce SAM to ethical issues too. Indeed, it is likely to have already been evaluating this question in parallel with the example we have talked through here.

This fictitious description of an AI called SAM is fraught with issues and problems and I have sought to acknowledge them along the way. I am very aware of the large number of practical issues that I have overlooked here but my intent and my hope is to illustrate how we could potentially use AI to automatically generate valuable new knowledge through discovery and test.

SAM also illustrates the point I made earlier about the need for us to think more broadly, beyond specific algorithms and models, and to consider how they integrate into a system that includes a range of functions that, collectively, can demonstrate useful, intelligence-like behaviour.

## AI and Cognitive Advantage

We are in a race to the top in terms of building a cognitive advantage. In the here and now the application of AI will be primarily in the 'doing things right' category of the wisdom hierarchy. But we will need to invest in AI that is able to reason at the higher levels of Pearl's hierarchy if we are to use machines to augment our own reasoning; the more we can get machines to think on our behalf, the greater our own cognitive capacity can be. Pursuing a general AI strategy as part of a R&D investment is therefore essential to building a cognitive advantage.

Any organisation that is serious about cognitive advantage needs to be investing in a general AI ideology, and by doing so, to be constantly exploring new and better ways to comprehend and act in its environment. Rather than seeing it as a waste of time, or even somehow unethical, pursuit of an AI investment strategy is the most effective way down the path that you need to tread anyway.

There is a cognitive gap between those companies that have adopted AI and those that haven't, and an organisation that gets behind the curve in the use of AI and data science will quickly reach the limits of its cognitive capacity. Its ability to comprehend the environment and act is seriously compromised, and every day that this continues unchecked, the more the gap widens.

AI is not optional anymore, and organisations that ignore it will fall behind fast. I suspect that the rate of being left behind is exponential. This differential in AI capabilities between rivals will be the cause of cognitive burden on the less well prepared.

If an organisation hasn't already invested in AI, it is urgent to do so. For thought leaders in this area – DeepMind, Facebook, Netflix, Amazon – it is time to think about the next stage: how to use what they are learning now – about managing application-specific AI – to augment and automate their human workforce, and move them up the wisdom hierarchy, to tap into the unique capacities of human intellect: sentiment, wisdom and creativity, assisted by artificial intellects.

However, this on its own does not lead to cognitive advantage. The development and operation of the cognitive enterprise, that is designed to optimise the fusion of artificial with human intellects to make better decisions, will also be key.

Cognitive advantage requires us to use AI to help us to continually make sense of our environment, to comprehend it accurately and to act with precision and clear intent. We need to engineer AI – or, more specifically, intelligent agents – to routinely evaluate what is happening in the world we are interested in; an intelligent agent needs to have the ability to infer causality from what it perceives, so that it can come up with hypotheses about why things happened, then test them, and then evaluate the results.

An intelligent agent can do a lot of the heavy lifting of discovering and recording new knowledge that we have confidence in. At least, it can generate sufficient confidence for us to evaluate and act in a timely manner. Humans are good at being curious, but we are slower, and thus limit the number of possibilities we can consider at any one time. An organisation that is on a cognitive advantage trajectory will need to use AI to constantly experiment, either in the environment itself or in a synthetic environment, in order to build as accurate a picture as possible of the causal architecture of the environment. Knowing causal architecture drives better decisions.

The better we understand the true power structure of our environment, the better able we are to come up with strategy and tactics; and given that we are in an arms-race against other organisations that are also using AI to do the same, this is a time-critical priority.

The ability of AI to operate at all levels of Pearl's 'Ladder of Causation' may result in an AI that becomes very powerful. I cannot yet conceive of what this means. But I do know we will need to set guiding principles by which our AI operates, and how we develop it. Knowing how to set those guiding principles requires foresight, to be able to imagine future scenarios based on the course we choose.

World-class institutions and companies are collaborating on exploring the ethics of AI, for example, the Royal Society of Arts partnering with DeepMind, to draw up an 'ethics toolkit for AI'. Whilst these guidelines are welcomed, they do not set out a fundamental and compelling principle for how we should engineer AI capabilities. For that, it may be worth considering a talk, given at the virtual Cheltenham Science Festival in June 2020, by the AI researcher, Stuart Russell.

Russell gave a talk on the ethics of AI. His proposition is simple: we should design AI to have one goal, which is to satisfy human preferences. Help humans to do what humans want to do. This doesn't involve telling AI what those preferences are – the key is that AI should be designed to figure out what those preferences are and seek to fulfil them.

This may be a way to set boundaries for AI, to make it safe, at a fundamental level. It is a simple principle: all AI should be designed with the goal of understanding and fulfilling human preferences. He has suggested a way to encode a good ethos into AI by designing a permanent principle that AI should follow. AI is programmed with a purpose that is aligned with human good.

It is a wonderful example of sagacious thinking although, of course, we would need to consider the very small minority of humans whose preferences we certainly would not want to perpetuate nor assist in our society.

The examples I have given in this chapter are just the beginning. The world is not simple. Most processes, either in nature or man-made, are non-linear, circular, convoluted, and oftentimes just plain random. Looking at even a moderately complex system and we soon realise that we can't point at any kind of causal direction; we don't know where causality may start.

If we cannot easily delineate the cause-and-effect of some event, or some system of interest, then we describe it as complex.

COGNITIVE ADVANTAGE

COGNITIVE ADVANTAGE

# Chapter 5

# Mastering Complexity

*'... the next century will be the century of complexity'*[27]

Stephen Hawking

In everyday language, we say that something is complex when we cannot easily understand its behaviour, 'Oh, it's just too complex, it's too confusing. I don't understand it!'. We struggle to understand the behaviour of something that is complex because it challenges our ability to delineate cause-and-effect – 'I push this and this happens'. If an action does not lead to the same response, each time you perform that action, then your understanding of the behaviour of that thing is uncertain. You cannot predict with 100% confidence how that thing will behave next.

The more uncertain we are about cause-and-effect, the more complex is the system we are attempting to understand. An ability to make sense of a complex situation, to identify the most beneficial and impactful action to take, and to have the agency to act with speed and accuracy to elicit that desired effect, is the main attribute required for building and maintaining a cognitive advantage.

A Newtonian view of the world – as an immensely complicated and predictable mechanical machine – does not help to explain complex behaviour. A reductionist approach to science – where you understand something by dismantling it into its constituent parts and scrutinising each individually – is woefully ill-equipped to explain emergent phenomena. As Stephen Hawking's quote at the beginning of this chapter suggests, many things simply cannot be explained from studying individual components.

## Emergence

One of the most striking and intuitive examples of a complex system can be found in nature – a flock of starlings murmuring where the simple rules that determine the interaction between birds generate complex patterns. We think we understand why starlings murmur, and there is a beautiful simplicity to it. Each bird is following a set of local rules:

   a.   I don't want to be on the outside of the flock because I'm more exposed to predators

   b.   I don't want to crash into the 6-7 birds that are closest to me

   c.   I don't want to hit the ground

Just following those three simple rules, at the same time as constantly making sense of their environment, their position, their flight path, how far they are from each other and whether they are on the outside of the flock or not, leads to the phenomenon of murmuring.

What makes this behaviour difficult to predict is the information processing that is occurring in the brain of each bird. If a bird moves to the left and its neighbour on that side moves to the right, the bird must make a correction. It doesn't continue going left. In the next cycle of its comprehension loop, it moves to the right. Where the bird moves next is a result of the behaviour of the flock, as well as any changes in the local environment, such as predators, undulating ground and obstacles.

Starlings are a lovely example because complexity arises much more readily from the interactions between things or objects. Whilst I have talked previously about cognition and autonomous behaviour of individuals, if there is one lesson I have learned from my own research into complexity, it is that when objects/entities start interacting with other objects/entities, their collective behaviour can get complex very quickly.

For us to begin to develop an understanding of a complex system we need to understand the relationships between the components that constitute the system. The interaction between elementary components (e.g., people) can give rise to intermediate forms (e.g., marketplaces) that generate high-level forms (e.g., cities, economies, climate). This 'bottom-up' flow can generate high-level forms that subsequently influence, or constrain, the behaviour of those lower-level forms that generated it (e.g., the formation of a biological membrane can change the behaviour of those internal chemical reactions that generated it) in a 'top-down' flow.

Autopoiesis, which I introduced in Chapter 3, is the simplest model of emergence that illustrates this bottom-up and top-down closure. Incidentally, this is why a reductionist approach to understanding complex systems is not sufficient: by understanding each component separately we miss the vital information gained by understanding the relationship between components and the phenomena that they can generate through their interactions. Another way to appreciate this is in the words of Carlo Rovelli, '… things don't have properties exclusive to themselves, their properties only exist by virtue of their relationship to other things…'[28]

Even though we might understand the simple rules that drive individual behaviour we cannot predict with any useful level of confidence how the shape of the flock, its direction of travel, and so on, will change from one moment to the next. Even if we were able to monitor the velocity and direction of travel of each bird, we would not be able to predict the future shape of the flock based on its present state.

There are two factors that prevent us from achieving this: knowability and determinability.

## Knowability

In 2002, Donald Rumsfeld (then the United States Secretary of Defence) gave a press briefing at the Pentagon where he uttered the now famous phrase:

'… as we know, there are known knowns; there are things we know we know. We also know there are known unknowns; that is to say we know there are some things we do not know. But there are also unknown unknowns – the ones we don't know we don't know'[29]

He only needed to mention unknown knowns and he would have had a full house.

Consider the following table:

| Unknown | Unknown knowns | Unknown unknowns |
|---|---|---|
| | There are things that we don't know that we know.<br><br>We understand some things, but we are not aware that we do understand them. | There are things that we don't know that we don't know.<br><br>We are neither aware of them nor do we understand them. |
| Known | Known knowns | Known Unknowns |
| | There are things that we know that we know.<br><br>We are aware of them and we understand them. | There are things that we know that we don't know.<br><br>There are things that we are aware of, but we do not understand them. |
| | Known | Unknown |

Table 3. The Knowability matrix.

Where our knowledge about a system resides in this matrix can be called our knowability of that system. There will be parts of the system that we know and understand, for example, the individual behaviour of each bird (at least, we have a good enough approximation of their behaviour). There will be parts of the system that we know we don't know, for example, what the shape of the formation of birds will be in 10 seconds time. And so on.

Of course, there are undoubtedly aspects to murmuring that we don't know we don't know. And, if the first paper on starling murmuration had never been published, then we would not know that we knew something about starlings.

If something – your neighbour, the economy, the weather – is knowable, it can be observed and understood. Knowability is the capability, or the permissiveness, of something to being observed and understood, and therefore to being known.

## Determinability

To determine means to understand something to the point where we can conclude something about it (based on the information we have available). We are determining on a cause leading to an effect. Determinability is the capability, or the permissiveness, of something to being determined in this way. A degree of knowability is a pre-requisite to determinability.

For example, a glass falls on the floor and shatters. I determine that it was my hand that knocked the glass off the counter thus causing it to fall to the floor. Determinability here is very high and we have a high level of confidence in our understanding of what caused the glass to break.

But now consider if we ask the question, 'Why did my elbow come into contact with the glass?' This is less obvious. Was I daydreaming? Was I distracted by something? Was I actually reaching for the glass but for whatever reason I fumbled the pick up? Did I stumble a bit? It is less easy to determine the cause here.

In trying to understand what happened here we are trying to associate a cause to an effect. We are using both our short-term memory (immediate recall of what happened and what immediately preceded the event) and our long-term memory (has this happened before and what did I learn about it at that time?) However, given that there is now a multiplicity of possible causes, our certainty about the primary cause is reduced. The more uncertainty we have about the causal relationships in a system, the more complex the system is.

## Defining Complexity

Complexity is the state of a system where our knowability of it and the determinability of it is such that we have uncertainty about our understanding of it. This uncertainty may be because we lack the means to explore the system in a meaningful and achievable way – to gather datapoints that may yield insights – or we may simply lack the common knowledge required to make sense of what we are observing. Having data in hand does not mean that the system that generated it can be understood. Consider the following:

**Low knowability and low determinability.** Human society. Humans are one of the most complex systems that we are aware of. Whether it is the advanced molecular machinery that keeps our cells functioning, or the billion-plus neurons in our brain, or simply the unpredictable nature of people. There is a *lot* going on inside a human that we cannot access and therefore do not know about.

Humans are continually adapting to what they have learned, heard or seen. We are constantly changing. What we are thinking from one moment to the next is hidden from direct and real-time observation. How we may behave from one moment to the next might follow a pattern, but occasionally we will change our behaviour in unpredictable ways. Those fundamental beliefs that drive our behaviour can change over time. Illness can affect us too.

**Low knowability but high determinability.** The internet. We have a very intricate understanding of how the internet works – through an interplay of different technical standards developed by humans – however our ability to be omniscient about what is currently happening across the internet is low. Our knowability is low due to the sheer scale of the internet, the fact that parts of the internet are not readily accessible, and so on.

**High knowability but low determinability.** The weather. We have a sophisticated array of instrumentation and data – from barometers, temperature, satellite imagery – to inform our understanding of what is currently happening with the weather. We also have models for understanding the formation of different weather patterns. Whilst we can predict the weather with increased confidence in the short term, this confidence fades as we attempt to predict further into the future. We do not have the ability to predict cause-and-effect much beyond the short-term of the next few hours or next few days.

**High knowability and high determinability.** An aeroplane. We have a very detailed understanding of how an aeroplane works and we have a very high level of knowledge about the state of the system (sensors, instrumentation, telemetry data) because we have designed in the capture of essential datapoints that we need to attain a high level of understanding of the system.

As such, a complex decision is one where we are seeking to identify the best outcome from our action even though we have uncertainty about our understanding of the system in which we are seeking to act. This uncertainty increases as our knowability and determinability of that system decreases. In such circumstances, our actions can become nothing more than informed guesswork. As such, a key imperative is to invest in tools and strategies that increase our knowability and our determinability of those complex systems that matter to us.

We are fortunate that we exist in a world that is becoming increasingly rich in data and computing resources (as described in Chapter 2), equipping us to better understand complex systems. Over the past 50 years, efforts have been made to develop tools, models and theories to help us understand complex systems. This accumulated set of tools and knowledge generated in the pursuit of untangling complexity is called complexity science.

## Complexity Science

Complexity science is an emerging, multidisciplinary field of scientists and engineers who seek to understand how large systems behave and change over time. A 'large system' is simply a collection of things that are somehow connected to each other. The more components that are involved, the larger the system.

Now, you may think that a Boeing 787 Dreamliner is a complex system, but it is not. It is a complicated system that consists of 2.3 million parts. Whilst our knowability of the state of each of those parts is low, our determinability of the behaviour of the system is high (and one of the motivations for embedding more sensors and digital technologies in aircraft is to yield more datapoints to increase our knowability).

Humans – with the aid of computers – have designed the system to operate with a very high degree of predictability across a wide range of scenarios. As a feat of engineering, it is hugely impressive. But the Dreamliner is not complex. For a Dreamliner to be deemed complex it would have to have degrees of freedom that allow it to generate novelty; that is, to create a state of operation that was not conceived of by an engineer.

However, the process of designing the Dreamliner was complex. Very complex. Why? Because it involved humans interacting with other humans in a convoluted dance of ideas, debate and decision. The idea that comes out of a design meeting may not have been at all predictable at the start of that meeting. This is because we adapt our thinking: to the ideas of others – some more so than others – and to what we are learning through such interactions.

We can also behave in an unpredictable way. We may have not slept well the night before, or we may be daydreaming about what it would feel like to finally be able to go on holiday. Such states of mind may either diminish or amplify our ability to undertake a task. Aeroplanes don't have off days.

Whilst human behaviour can be predictable – we are creatures of habit after all and we also, overall, tend to react similarly to external stimuli – we can often be unpredictable too.

Predicting the future behaviour of a complex system can be challenging because they adapt and change over time. Being adaptable – with the characteristic of unpredictability that this elicits – is the hallmark of complexity. With complexity science we are interested in how large adaptive systems (artificial or natural) change over time.

## Open-Endedness and Novelty

A system that is open-ended has no pre-determined limits. Biological evolution is a good example of an open-ended system that generates novelty over time. The constant plethora of new products and services produced daily in our economy is another example. Trying to understand an open-ended system with a view to predicting what may happen next is extremely difficult and, pragmatically, not necessarily desirable.

The main feature of open-endedness is the generation of novelty, that is, where new forms are created within the system. These new forms then begin to interact members of that system, thus changing the system that generated them. The scale of this change may be significant (for example, the mutation of a virus that gives it greater transmissibility) or insignificant (for example, the creation of a new iPhone app that fails to gain any users).

Novelty can increase our uncertainty about a system as it adds to the number of possible causes of the behaviour of the system. Conversely, it may decrease uncertainty in a system; for example, the adoption of an industry standard (such as the Blu-Ray standard) can reduce uncertainty for consumers, thus leading to the creation of a new market (whilst, in the process, creating more short-term uncertainty for those operating in that market).

The sharp-eyed amongst you will have noted that the effect of novelty can move an ecosystem either towards or away from its window of viability (as discussed in Chapter 3).

Unpredictability can arise because the interactions occurring within a complex system generate something new, unexpected, unusual or original. Consider this example of a hypothetical conversation with a friend after watching a film at the local cinema:

Me:     Well, it was a great plot, but the acting was pretty shocking

Friend: Really? Oh, I thought the acting was great

Me:     No way. Why would you think that?

Friend: Because the main character was based on a real person, and that is how that person behaved in real life. They were famous for it!

Me:     Oh wow, I did not know that. I'll have to check that out.

Now, okay, not the most exciting of stories but this does illustrate the following important points:

1)  I could not have predicted how this conversation ended. Indeed, I would have been very surprised by the outcome

2)  It shows the effect lack of knowledge can have on our ability to accurately perceive events and to make a correct (or, at least, a less

wrong) interpretation

3) Interacting with others can generate new knowledge and can also influence, or shape, beliefs (my friend changed my belief that the film was pretty rubbish)

Now, complexity science cannot remove the uncertainty of such situations. But it can provide an explanation for the changing state of such situations. In this example I was sharing my belief about something with my friend who, in turn, shared their belief with me. In doing so they changed my belief. I adapted my belief model.

This forming the beliefs of others and having our own beliefs formed by others is a continuous process called dialectics (which I discuss more in Chapter 5).

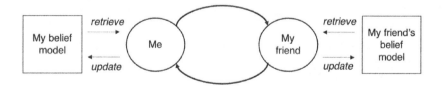

*Figure 7. Through our interactions with people, we share our beliefs about the world. In doing so we open ourselves up to having our beliefs changed or reinforced as we gain new knowledge and insight.*

Figure 7 illustrates a simple feedback loop. I say something to you, you make sense of that, attach a meaning to it, and you act. I perceive your actions and that may, or may not, influence my next action. However, occasionally you may surprise me. When you do, I will start to divert more of my conscious brain to make sense of this surprise. 'What does this mean? I wasn't expecting this. Is this a good or a bad thing?' and so on. Depending on how I interpret this surprising event – which will be a function of my current state of mind, my personality type, how tired I am – I may update my belief model about the world.

Figure 7 also introduces a common notation used in capturing the structure of a complex system: a graph (or network). Each object in the system can be represented as a node in this network (the circles) and the directed arrows (links) that connect the nodes signify that there is a relationship between those two nodes e.g., a flow of information, material or causation. Even in the simple network shown here, one thing should be clear: my influencing of you changes your behaviour which, in turn, may influence me.

This circularity is called a feedback loop – which we'll come onto shortly – and it is one of the main structural elements of a complex system. So, whilst novelty can arise through the interactions between components, novelty can also arise through randomness.

## Randomness

Randomness is a behaviour that lacks any discernible pattern and so we could not have predicted its occurrence and nor could we subsequently predict any future occurrence. A visual example of randomness is the 'random walk as shown in Figure 8.

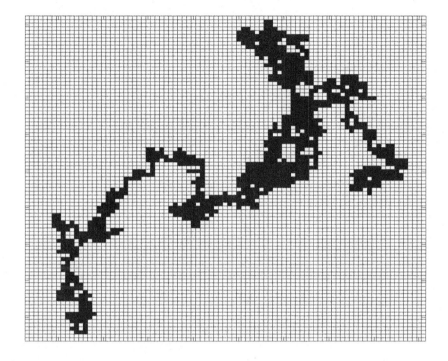

*Figure 8. The result of a simulation of a random walk. As can be seen, there are no distinguishable patterns evident in the trail left by the walker. Random walker simulation on a 100 x 100 grid environment developed by the author in Matlab.*

The walker starts in a central position on a square grid. At each moment in time the walker chooses whether to go North, South, East or West with equal chance of ¼, ¼, ¼, ¼. Each grid location that the walker visits is set to the colour black allowing us to track the movement of the walker.

Over time the path that the walker has created lacks any discernible pattern (as can be seen in Figure 8). If I were to ask you, 'Where do you think the walker will move next?' (let's assume the walker is in the bottom left of the grid) you would only be able to give me an answer with 25% confidence;

and if I were to ask you where you think the walker would be after another ten moves, you would not be able to tell me with any certainty at all – and you might refuse blank to answer my question on the grounds of futility.

If you were game, then you might say 'The walker might be here, or here'. The point is, you would be giving me a likelihood of where the walker might be; but you would have little confidence and this level of confidence would diminish the further into the future I asked you to predict.

Fortunately, complex systems are not random and so they are more susceptible to analysis and understanding. Indeed, the formation of repeatable patterns allows a complex system to endure over time; but they may also exhibit randomness, and this could nudge the system into a new state of operation, or it may have no effect at all. Complex systems have the *potential* for randomness which may lead to novel forms or events that perturb the system into a completely new state, thus allowing it to adapt over time. Evolution and genetics have taught us this.

The ability to adapt gives complex systems the intrinsic characteristic of non-linearity.

## Non-Linearity and Feedback Loops

Non-linear is not an intuitive term. At least, when I first encountered it, I didn't think so. The simplest way that I have found to explain non-linearity is by looking at the output from two simple equations (do not worry about the meaning of the equations – they are just for illustration):

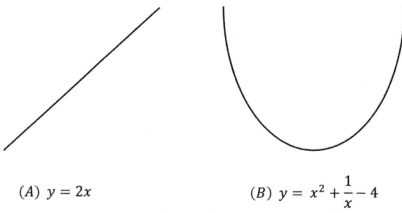

$$(A) \; y = 2x \qquad\qquad (B) \; y = x^2 + \frac{1}{x} - 4$$

*(A) is a linear equation. As we change the input (x) then the output (y) changes by a constant amount. Plotting the output of this equation on a graph, for increasing values of x, the output increases at a constant gradient, thus forming a straight line. The rate of change in y is constant and the graph is a straight line, hence we call this a linear equation; for example, every week my daughter saves a quarter of her pocket money.*

*(B) is a non-linear equation. As we change the input (x), the output (y) changes by a varying amount. The rate of change in y is continuously changing. Plotting the output of this equation on a graph, for increasing values of x, the gradient of the line, and the direction of the gradient, is variable, as depicted by the arc shown. The output of the equation is not linear – hence non-linear, for example, the motion of a pendulum swing.*

A system is said to be non-linear if the output from the system is not proportional to the input to the system. Because the output is not proportional to the input it can be difficult to predict how the system is going to change over time. We have uncertainty over cause (input) and effect (output).

Hence, nonlinear systems tend to exhibit complex behaviour. What is more, nonlinear behaviour can have a big impact. Putting aside the quixotic notion of a butterfly flapping its wings in the Amazon rainforest and causing a hurricane in Florida, one of the main characteristic behaviours of non-linearity is that a small change in the input to a system can cause a large change at the output to the system.

Consider the anti-government protests in the Arab world that started in the early 2010s, known as the 'Arab Spring'. Whilst there is no doubt that a multitude of factors contributed to creating the conditions for an uprising, the tipping point came in Egypt when a photo of Khaled Mohamed Saeed's body (who died whilst in police custody) spread over social media platforms and lit the Egyptian revolution. That small action – posting a photo on social media, which happens millions of times a day across the world – led to the downfall of a government.

The complex system of social media – with people sharing and discussing the photo – had a massive amplifying effect that then played out in the real world, in the form of protests and demonstrations. This 'network effect' of social media has also been seen more recently, with the death of George Floyd whilst being arrested in the United States and the murder of Sarah Everard in the UK.

Non-linear equations are hard to solve and there are very few that can be solved using traditional mathematical analysis techniques. There is an entire field of mathematics – nonlinear dynamics – dedicated to analysing non-linear systems and for the reader who is interested in finding out more I thoroughly recommend Steve Strogatz's classic book called, unsurprisingly, 'Nonlinear Dynamics'.

The main point to take away about non-linearity is this: because the output of a system varies, it can be difficult to predict what it will do next. This variability is generated by the structure and flows within the complex system. Any system that we may be interested in is likely to have many components that are interacting with each other. The output from one component ($x$) feeds into another component ($y$) whose output may be an input to ($x$).

Such feedback loops can generate non-linearities which, as we now know, leads to an output from a system that cannot be pre-determined, or necessarily predicted, from inputs to the system. The *effect* of such feedback loops can sometimes be understood as positive (where they amplify an effect) or negative (where they dampen an effect).

With climate change, for example, what is causing the glaciers to melt? Is it because of $CO_2$ or is it just a natural weather effect? Statistics would suggest the former but, so far, have not proven compelling enough to lead to definitive, unified action. We need to get beyond the data – measurements of $CO_2$, sea temperatures, and so on –to understand the complex web of cause-and-effect that is driving our climate.

To reveal just some of the surprising insights that complexity science can yield about the impact of public policy on climate change, research by Natalie Mahowald – an Engineering Professor at Cornell University – and colleagues revealed the paradoxical situation whereby China is responsible for both heating up ($CO_2$ emissions) and cooling down (aerosol emissions) global temperatures.

As such, the somewhat surprising observation is that they may be, arguably, offsetting their contribution to global warming through their continued high usage of aerosols (which were subject to a widespread ban by Western governments two decades ago). Is the current global policy on climate change too narrowly focused on $CO_2$ or, even more alarmingly, driven by science that is woefully ill-equipped to sufficiently support policy makers?

When there are hundreds, even thousands, of possible causes for one effect, and that effect has a feedback loop, so it could be modulating in some way the processes that also cause it, then we get into incredibly difficult analytical territory. It becomes even more complex to draw out the causal architecture of the environment when that environment is constantly changing, which it always is. A huge amount of sophisticated data processing is required.

It looks overwhelmingly complicated from where we are now, but these kinds of challenges can be engineered.

This is the purpose of the cognitive enterprise. It is designed to manage that complexity, to be sufficiently fast at performing causal analysis of complex systems, and then – most importantly – conveying that knowledge and understanding to both artificial and human intellects such that it aids comprehension of the environment, how it might be changing and what we should be doing about it.

**Positive Feedback Loop.** A positive feedback loop moves a system away from its initial state: in this example, the state of sea ice is diminishing over time. Figure 9 illustrates the relationship between Arctic sea ice and global warming as an example of a positive feedback loop in a complex system.

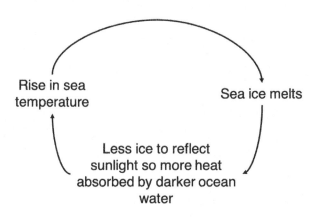

*Figure 9. Illustration of the phenomena of melting sea as a positive feedback loop*

**Negative feedback loop.** A negative feedback loop counteracts a change to return a system to a previous (and desired) state. Homeostasis is often used as an example of a negative feedback loop. Our body seeks to maintain a constant internal temperature of 37.4° C. As our temperature deviates from this we either start sweating or we start shivering. Those actions have the effect of decreasing or increasing our temperature to get it back into normal range.

Understanding the main characteristics of a complex system, so that you have a sufficient understanding of *how* the system behaves, is more likely to yield a useful insight compared to spending time building an intricate model in exceptionally precise detail, if it does not elicit additional and valuable insight.

But this can be a chicken-and-egg problem. How do we know what is the right question to ask, to yield sufficient insight to allow us to comprehend a complex system sufficiently that we can decide how to act? This conundrum is affectionately known as 'cutting the Gordian knot'.

## Cutting the Gordian Knot

The Gordian Knot is a historical reference to a (probably apocryphal) story about Alexander the Great solving a puzzle of how to untie a complex knot without cutting any of the cords. Legend has it that this knot was so complex and intricate that it was not possible to tell where to even begin. Alexander solved the problem by using his sword to cut the stays on which the knot was held, thus allowing him to unravel the knot without damaging any of the rope.

Nowadays, 'cutting the Gordian knot' – admittedly, untying or unravelling may be more accurate depictions – has come to be used as a metaphor for grappling with a seemingly intractable problem, that may yet hold a simple and elegant solution if only one could figure it out.

Alexander the Great's considerations extended only to the simple act of unravelling the intricate knot. The hard, knotty problems that are faced today by leaders in government, industry and academia extend beyond the immediate problem in hand to the whole range of possible consequences that may unfold from solving the problem.

For example, could Boris Johnson – the British Prime Minister during the Covid-19 global pandemic – have foreseen that solving the problem of getting the 'R number' (retransmission rate) below one, to reduce the spread of coronavirus, would have had such widespread ramifications on society and the economy?

This challenge is also the opportunity to get ahead of the competition and adversaries – how to devise an elegant solution to the first order problem, and devise elegant solutions for the second-, third-, $n$-th order consequences that may arise from solving the first order problem.

This formidable challenge requires pioneers with the determination and ingenuity to embrace the tremendous consequent opportunity. Indeed, given the increasing complexity of the world in which we live (as I outlined in Chapter 2), leaders of major organisations may not even have a choice of whether to develop skills and resources for complex decision-making.

This quality of decision-making we are alluding to here – to not only understand the immediate problem, but also the likely cascade of consequences that unfurl from that – can be thought of as acting with sagacity.

Sagacity means to have a keen, penetrative insight to a complex situation, and that insight leading to wise and holistic action. For the rest of this chapter, I will share with you my thoughts on the tools and the technologies we can orchestrate, to equip every human in an organisation with the means to act with sagacity – reliably, ethically and at pace.

In other words: sagacity = maximum cognitive performance.

## Engineering for Maximum Cognitive Performance

When BAE Systems, Airbus and Leonardo began development of the Eurofighter Typhoon aircraft, their engineers didn't ask the question 'How do we make this the best plane to fly?' They asked, 'How do we design this plane so that the pilot can focus on achieving their mission?' They recognised that the pilot needed more time to make sense of the considerable amount of information that was hitting them from multiple sources simultaneously.

By integrating information from different sensor systems on the aircraft and presenting that in an intuitive way to the pilot, rather than leave it to the pilot to do that information processing, the pilot could gain critical and timely insight to what their adversary was doing, what allied troops on the ground were doing, and so on.

Of course, the pilot needed to be trained to interpret and use such information. Indeed, the pilot was considered the centrepiece of this complex system. The more recent Joint Strike Fighter aircraft goes a step further by using AI to recommend courses of action to the pilot, for example, suggesting the order in which the pilot neutralises enemy ground threat positions.

The focus was on understanding where the human could make the best contribution to mission success (i.e., mission management), and then to design and engineer the system around achieving that goal (i.e., automation of many of the avionic systems required to keep the plane in the air). We now have the opportunity – courtesy of accessible, scalable and affordable computing platforms – to apply a similar engineering ethos that places the decision-maker (e.g., a politician, a CEO, a doctor, and so on) as the key focus in designing a system. Such a decision-centric, or intellect-centric, approach is a powerful way to design jobs, tools and support systems in an organisation, including where AI is itself the decision-maker.

Previously, I introduced the notion of the *cognitive agent,* as encompassing both humans and machines that undertake cognitive information processing functions – for example, perception, pattern recognition, reasoning, imagining, and so on. Hence, whilst I have used the example of a system engineered around the human, you could equally swap out the human and replace them with a machine.

The design goal remains the same: to maximise the cognitive performance of the *cognitive agent* in making a good decision, an optimal choice in the pursuit of a goal. (For ease of comprehension and continuity in this chapter I will continue to take a human perspective on complex decision-making, rather than the more prosaic notion of a cognitive agent). I discuss the concept of a cognitive agent in more detail in Chapter 8.

Our ability to make sense of a complex situation, to identify the most beneficial and impactful action to take, and to have the agency to act with speed and accuracy to elicit the desired effect, is the main attribute required for building and maintaining a cognitive advantage.

So far in this book, and particularly so in this chapter, I have outlined the role of artificial intelligence, synthetic environments, and complexity science. I have intentionally not been exhaustive in my examination of any of these subjects, merely wishing to describe them sufficiently for the reader to understand their utility. Nevertheless, it is in the seamless integration of these three areas that a cognitive advantage – for the individual and for the organisation - can be built and maintained.

Consider again the 'wisdom of hierarchy' that I introduced in Chapter 3 with some additional annotations (and as per Figure 10).

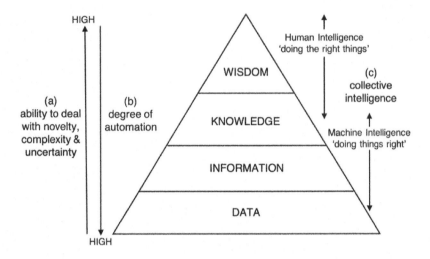

*Figure 10. An enhanced version of the 'wisdom hierarchy' to show how the use of AI and other digital tools such as Digital Twins and Synthetic Environments should be engineered to maximise a human's cognitive performance in undertaking a complex task or decision.*

Where:

a)   The use of AI, synthetic environments and digital tools to *augment* and help humans deal with novel, complex and highly uncertain situations with the aim of reaching a good decision. I will discuss synthetic environments shortly.

b)   The use of AI and other techniques to *automate* the processing of data and information, thus relieving the human – and other AI – from the task. This frees up the human to focus on contextualising knowledge and experience to gain deep insight to a situation.

c) The use of AI and human intelligence in a *collaborative* and collective manner to excel at causal reasoning in a fluid, seamless and harmonious manner, where humans focus on answering questions on, 'doing the right things', whilst AI focuses on 'doing things right'.

The integration of these three – automation, augmentation and collaboration – should significantly increase the cognitive performance of the human (or, more generally, the cognitive agent).

## Simulating Complex Systems

Complexity science is, by necessity, a multidisciplinary endeavour. Any system of interest can be looked at through a number of different lenses: an information processing lens, a physical lens, a chemical lens, a social lens, and so on. Or, to put these lenses into more technical terms: a network, a graphical probabilistic model, an agent-based model, a reaction graph.

The simultaneous use of multiple lenses is the key to unlocking the secrets of a complex system. Wouldn't it be great if we had one tool that would allow us to switch easily between these different lenses? Fortunately, we do, and it is called a computer simulation.

A computer simulation is a synthetic representation of a system that may, or may not, exist in the real world. This system could be modelling climate change, global weather patterns, the world economy, stock markets, and so on. Or it could be an environment where intelligent agents (whether AI or humans) interact to play games such as Go or Chess. Or it could be more specialised and intricate simulations, such as a flight simulation, modelling the engine of a Formula 1 racing car (McLaren), the electrical activity of a human heart (University of Oxford), or the operation of an oil well (BP/Palantir).

For example, in more recent years the terms 'digital twin' and 'synthetic environment' have been used to describe high-fidelity computer simulations of real-world systems. Incidentally, virtual worlds, or artificial worlds – such as massively online multiplayer games like Fortnite – have a significant role to play in helping us to discover new knowledge. However, for the purposes of this chapter, I focus more on virtual environments that are simulations of real-world systems.

**Digital Twin**

A digital twin is a high-fidelity and faithful digital representation of a physical system. Data is collected from the physical system to update the digital twin in real-time (or near real-time depending on the application). Algorithms running on the digital twin can then be used to do automated control, anomaly detection and so on.

An 'offline' version of a digital twin can help engineers and managers to explore future scenarios through simulating different possible states of operation of the complex system and subsequent likely outcomes from taking certain courses of action (a colleague of mine uses the wonderful term, 'a cascade of consequences', to capture this point).

The range of applications for digital twins is potentially vast, although economic (affordability), social (ethics of how data is collected, processed and stored) and technological factors (access to sufficient computing and storage capacity and resilient architectures) have a modulating effect on what can be achieved.

**Synthetic Environment**

A synthetic environment is defined as a very large-scale and highly realistic computer simulation of large systems of interest. Synthetic environments are usually heterogeneous; they make use of multiple models and data sources integrated in a way that is accessible, discoverable and manipulable by a user. For example, combining weather patterns, traffic monitoring and air quality measurements to predict pollution levels in a city throughout the day.

Another example, the different theatres of war across air, naval and ground forces could be simulated in near real-time, and this information presented to key decision-makers (e.g., the United Kingdom's Ministry of Defence Single Synthetic Environment technology demonstrator).

**The relationship between Digital Twins and Synthetic Environments**

The question that often arises in conversations I have with colleagues and acquaintances is - what is the difference between a digital twin and a synthetic environment? I advocate for the following: a synthetic environment may consist of, or make use of, a number of digital twins (possibly a large number) to achieve its scale of realism.

A digital twin may be used within multiple synthetic environments. There is a many-to-many relationship between synthetic environments and digital twins. I tend, somewhat simplistically, to envisage digital twins as the high integrity and high-fidelity building blocks of synthetic environments.

As a budding software engineer, I had drilled into me the importance of always striking the right balance between the cohesion of the code that I was writing (its ability to run with minimal reliance on other separate blocks of code) and the coupling of that code to other blocks of code. The term *modularity* conveys this notion of good software engineering and I believe it remains very relevant to how we engineer synthetic environments and digital twins.

I propose that synthetic environments should excel at integrating numerous models, simulations, algorithms and data that are available within an ecosystem into a seamless experience, through effective human-machine interface design, for a user seeking to develop a rational, intuitive and profoundly deep insight into a complex system. Meanwhile digital twins should excel at being high-fidelity, efficient and robust with high degrees of internal cohesion. Both should be founded on a secure, high-trust, end-to-end data and technology stack.

I believe the distinction between digital twins and synthetic environments should help us to delineate our goals as we design and engineer these incredibly sophisticated capabilities. For example, a synthetic environment could set out standards for ensuring interoperability between digital twins. Furthermore, these synthetic environments may exist within an ecosystem of other synthetic environments in an incomprehensibly sophisticated system-of-systems.

This is not a fantasy. In 2018 the National Digital Twin programme in the UK published its Gemini Principles, setting out how such an ecosystem could not only come to exist, but to thrive. By comparison, whilst a digital twin may need to be compatible with interoperable standards, that is not its main purpose.

The underlying architecture and standards used in developing and operating synthetic environments and digital twins should aim to create a trusted ecosystem that encodes privacy, security and verification (or possibly even certification) into its very fabric whilst also seeking to maximise the openness, inter-operability and accessibility of its constituent members.

**Simulating Complex Systems**

Complexity scientists were early adopters of computer simulations, back in the 1970s. The ability to simulate a complex entity consisting of many interacting components was a problem looking for a solution. A computer simulation makes it possible to model a complex system.

From observing how a complex system behaves in a computer simulation, we can begin to build a deeper understanding of the different states that the system can, or may, operate in. We may perturb the system to see how it reacts to different stimuli. We are experimenting. We are doing science. As we further develop the model, and our understanding of it, we can begin to bring in real-world data to validate and verify the model itself, whilst also learning more about the real-world system we are modelling.

At some point we may decide that we have gleaned as much knowledge as we need from the simulated version of a complex system; now it is time to expend the more expensive, more complex (and potentially messy) effort of experimenting in the real world. Of course, as we do this, we need to ensure that we put in place the right digital traces to capture datapoints that we can subsequently use to calibrate the parameters of our simulation. The feedback loop from the real-world into the simulated world is critical to validating and verifying the simulation model.

But how deep and detailed do these computer simulations need to be? And what can be realistically modelled with sufficient confidence that we can make high-stakes decisions based on any insight that can be gained? Let's take the hardest system to understand – humans.

Consider for a moment how difficult it would be to analyse a human to the extent that we are able to predict with high accuracy what they will do next. We don't yet have the means to do this, but we can look at a person's previous behaviours and actions – their history – and determine what they are likely to do next, based on their present situation (Facebook, Instagram, Google, Microsoft have developed so-called persuasion technology to pursue exactly this question). Apart from the ethical concerns this raises, we only end up with an approximate sense of what they may do next.

Now consider how to predict how two humans will behave whilst they are interacting. Think back to my earlier example of my friend and me leaving the cinema. We have emergent behaviour here through a dialectic.

Now consider how people behave in crowds. We have emergent behaviour that resembles flocking or herding patterns.

Now imagine trying to simulate an entire economy where millions of humans are making decisions and acting independently and sometimes collectively in real-time. Whilst fields of research such as Behavioural Economics are pursuing such a goal, I am not sure we will ever need, want, or even be able to achieve, a model of a complex system that has such detail and fidelity.

The point here is to illustrate how quickly things can become complex as we increase the scope and scale of the system that we are seeking to understand. Examining detail at too fine a level – modelling each individual human – may not yield much insight if we wish to understand the effect of climate change policies. But modelling the influence that those humans have on each other, and which can lead to more complex but also surprising behaviours, could yield rich and valuable insights.

Our challenge as complexity scientists, systems engineers and simulation designers is to determine what is a good enough level of detail to yield the insights needed to inform a decision. Therefore, a human-centric (or cognitive agent-centric) approach must be the starting point when designing simulations.

One way to get a feel for where we might go with developing convincing user experiences is to study the videogames industry. Games like Sid Meier's Civilisation – where you can build and run a marauding empire across the world – allow players to move seamlessly from different levels of information (from looking at how much food is in the town's cellars to the numbers of archers in an enemy formation), to different modes of operating (trade vs war), all whilst trying to stop their local citizens rioting when they set taxes too high. Games like Civilisation are both challenging and rewarding, and they are very addictive and compelling.

However, the secret of the success of these games is not just about the concept, the graphics and the game mechanics – although they are important – it is also about the human-machine interface. How the game interface has been designed is arguably the most important element of a videogame. If the controls are not intuitive, too complicated, or unreliable, then the magical 'suspension of disbelief' that any good game designer seeks will be absent. A good game designer also seeks to balance the mechanics so that it is neither too easy to finish nor too difficult, too early in the game, thus ensuring that the game has longevity and lasting appeal to the gamer.

In most complex systems simulations that I have used, or built, the user experience has been a secondary, even a tertiary, consideration. If, indeed, it has been considered at all. This is a significant blocker to complex systems simulations going mainstream and yet, as far as I am aware, there is little concerted effort to professionalise and commercialise this area (notable exceptions are companies like Palantir and Improbable).

I believe there are three reasons for this:

(i)   most computer simulations focus on accuracy first and foremost

(ii)  we do not have a common platform for simulations and, therefore, most of the time and effort of the designer of a simulation is spent 'reinventing the wheel' every time

(iii) people who are good at designing accurate and useful simulations are not necessarily good at understanding how a non-specialist user may be able to make use of that simulation

Videogames focus on giving players an utterly compelling experience where they are lost in a virtual world for a time. We need to reproduce that same depth of immersion in the field of complex systems simulations. So, simulation companies either need to transition their product into a platform that other developers and designers can work with – particularly those who are more experienced in human-machine interface design – or they need to develop in-house design skills.

The emerging fields of augmented reality, virtual reality, natural language processing, low power and flexible display technologies, sensors embedded in fabrics and haptics, all have the potential to revolutionise the human-machine interface. The scene in the film Minority Report, where the actor Tom Cruise is using gloves and special glasses to efficiently navigate a rich source of data and evidence to solve a crime, will look somewhat outdated and unambitious.

Another area where complex systems simulations are, at present, inadequate is in the lack of professionalisation of the software engineering practices that have been used to build the simulations. How has the underlying simulation software been tested? What assurances can the developers give that the simulation is generating expected and accurate results?

In June 2020, the British Computer Society published an article that raised the lack of professional practices in computer models and simulations as a serious impediment to their utility in guiding government policy. Their motivation was quite simple: the UK government were making high stakes decisions about the lockdown of the nation based in part on epidemiological models developed by academics that in no way are regulated nor is there an expectation in the academic community that the underlying algorithms that were running the epidemiological model should adhere to professional software engineering practices.

If we were to reflect on that for a moment: how would you feel about boarding a commercial flight across the Atlantic if you knew that the flight control algorithms had not been developed to any recognised engineering standard? Now you wouldn't have necessarily thought about this too much because the aviation industry is regulated. Let me ask how you would feel travelling in a self-driving car at 70mph in rain and heavy traffic, if you knew that the car's self-driving algorithms did not meet an industry standard for good real-time software design practices?

As we use computer simulations more and more – and this is already happening, look at how many countries are now developing a National Digital Twin, the UK included – such assurances of how the simulation has been built and validated will become as important as knowing that the prescription medicine you are taking has passed regulatory approval. After all, computer simulations – and I will extend this to include sophisticated algorithms that are modelling decision-making processes – will suggest outcomes that affect not only one or two people (e.g., should they receive mental health support?), nor entire nations (e.g., Covid-19 lockdown rules), but possibly the entire world (e.g., climate change policy).

Simulations give us the ability to explore, experiment and discover at a time and a place to suit us. Simulations can also fuse real-time data feeds directly into a virtual world, thus turning a simulation into a situational awareness tool.

The potential here is very substantial and investors have been taking notice. Several high-profile investors – Softbank, Andreesen Horowitz, Horizon Ventures and NetEase – have invested over $600m in a relatively young company called Improbable. Founded by two Cambridge University graduates, Herman Narula and Rob Whitehead, in 2012, Improbable markets itself as a gaming company. But, more crucially, it also markets itself as a platform for other people's very large-scale simulations, as well as massively multiplayer online games.

Improbable are building a platform to host other people's simulations, and their efforts should help to usher in greater standardisation which will be critical to the future of this field.

## How Does Simulating Complex Systems Build a Cognitive Advantage?

Firstly, it allows humans – through an effective human-machine interface – to engage intuitively with rich sources of data and knowledge. We can conceive of a user flowing from one concept to another, retrieving data from one repository, tasking an AI (by voice just as we do now with Alexa or Siri) to retrieve all related records in the organisation's knowledge repository; and all the time with real-time information fed into this virtual world. Switching operating modes, and now the human operator is planning possible moves and tactics to act in this environment.

Through trial-and-error, the human operator begins to get a feel for how a complex situation (for example, spending on advertising a new product) may play out under various parameters. The simulation is sufficiently sophisticated that as these scenarios are played out, they are convincing and credible. And they are quick. Time is accelerated. Parameters can be set to simulate different states of the operating environment – steady or turbulent – thus seeing how a set of strategies may play out where there is less data available.

Sometimes we may not have access to the data we need – so we synthesise the data; but we don't make it up. We have had an intelligent agent examining historical data to recognise patterns, variations, and so on, to the point where it can mimic that data in a simulation. Hence, even in the absence of data, future scenarios can be played out and understood, alternative strategies tried out, and so on. All before any action is made in the real world. All of this done by a trained human operator – a chief executive officer, a marketing manager, a customer service representative – in a way that, to most observers, would not look too different from their playing a videogame. This, at least, is one way that our future may unfold.

Secondly, an intelligent agent can also use the same simulation. An AI may not necessarily be seeking to answer the same questions as a human, and indeed, it may be fulfilling a question that has been posed by a human. But it should be offered the same experience, the same visuals, and access to the same repositories.

AI can use the simulation – or synthetic environment – to perform experiments very quickly, generating large amounts of data, analysing that data, then updating the semantic graph as the understanding of the environment changes, as played out in the simulation. Then new hypotheses could be generated from that new knowledge, and new understanding of the causal architecture of a system of interest could be furthered.

Government and industry may determine that certain applications of AI should be regulated. Such regulations may stipulate that an application-specific AI cannot be deployed in the real world until its full scale of actions have been tested and examined in a synthetic environment, and where the results yield a 95% confidence interval that the AI's operation is within specification. We need a safe space for AI to experiment and get it wrong. Synthetic environments will be fundamental to, and an enabler of, AI capabilities that need to be regulated.

Incidentally, this idea of AI using a simulation to prepare itself for acting in the real-world is not new. Tesla Inc. have been using computer simulations to train their 'Autopilot' neural network for years. Quite simply, they had to do this because their strategy was to pursue a self-driving car capability, even though they had very few cars on roads gathering real-time data. They used a synthetic environment to plug that data gap. Synthetic data can be extremely valuable in situations where access to real data is challenging or the data simply does not exist yet.

Within the context of Pearl's Ladder of Causation, and when we are problem-solving at the level of 'Counterfactuals' and 'Interventions', a dearth of data is likely to occur often. Hence, synthetic data that can be analysed and understood within a synthetic environment will be a significant catalyst for operating at the higher levels of reasoning from which deep insight and foresight is drawn.

Building a cognitive advantage is the application of a collective intelligence

– AI and humans – in understanding and acting seamlessly across synthetic and real environments. I propose that such learning is captured in two corporate assets: a semantic graph and a structural causal model. Maintaining these to such an accurate degree as to be a sufficient model of the environment, and the organisation's position in that environment, does not come without a cost.

So, it would serve us well to be circumspect about where we deploy our intelligent agents. For example, a digital organisation – with digital services and products, fully engaging with customers and partners in the digital economy – will generate a significant amount of data. The value of this data will vary significantly. Most of it will be low value, some of it will be extremely valuable. As part of a data strategy – defining what data we need, and where we get it from – we may have an expectation of the value of data dependent on its source. Determining what data is valuable, and therefore worth collecting and processing, needs to be explored carefully.

What if the environment is about to undergo a significant change, of which we are not yet aware? What if there are weak digital traces of this emerging change in the lower value data feeds that an organisation has access to but not actively analysing nor acting on?

In other words, how do we spot unknown unknowns and convert them to known unknowns? How do we sense emergent change in our environment whilst the change itself has yet to completely form?

We need an early warning system; a capability that can sniff, or parse, all our data feeds and detect new patterns that may signal the emergence of a new state of the environment. Complexity science (and I include computer simulations in that definition) combined with AI may give us such a capability.

## AI and Complexity

There are two ways in which AI and complexity are connected. In a phenomenological sense, AI significantly adds to the complexity of our world. Billions upon billions of automated actions taking place simultaneously – alongside those happening in the natural, physical world – can only serve to increase the maelstrom of uncertainty over what is causing what.

In a practical sense, though, AI will also help us to understand complex systems. Deep Learning is superb at pattern recognition. Deep Reinforcement Learning is superb at discovery. Neuro-symbolic networks may soon prove to be effective at inferring causation.

These are powerful tools to unlock the secrets of complex systems. AI also has a role to play in computer simulations to help humans, and other AI, play out possible scenarios to inform decision-making.

The role of AI in helping humans to deal with more complexity is to automate the acquisition and discovery of new knowledge. Or, referring to the previous section on knowability, AI can turn our unknowns into knowns.

**Known Knowns (KK).** We know the right things to do, we just need to do those things right and do them efficiently. AI can help to commoditise knowledge and decision-making in Known Knowns. AI makes decision-making here cheaper and faster than humans are able. Our understanding of cause-and-effect is sufficiently understood that the decision required for a given situation is obvious and simple. Automation is the main application of AI here. Full automation/autonomy of decisions are possible depending on the impact of an erroneous decision.

Decisions that deal with the 'known known' are low cost. We have a high confidence in the outcome of our actions. AI can make decisions in this space faster, cheaper and more accurately than humans, or it can assist humans to make decisions.

**Known Unknowns (KU).** We know that a thing exists, but we do not have enough information about it. We know the questions to ask, but we are unable to gather the information we need to answer those questions. AI can help with searching for data and information.

Decisions that deal with 'known unknowns' are driven by hypothesis testing. We believe we understand something, but we don't yet have evidence to prove or disprove whether we are correct. Decisions are based on probability of outcomes. AI can help to explore and discover new knowledge leading to new understanding (automated knowledge discovery) e.g., DeepMind's AlphaFold protein folding algorithm.

**Unknown knowns (UK).** Information that a person or an organisation has in its possession but whose existence and value has not been realised e.g., the deep expertise of an individual who subsequently leaves the organisation. Knowledge management is helpful here to turn these into known knowns. Crowd sourcing is another good example.

AI can help with automatically capturing knowledge about knowledge in an information management solution. Decisions that deal with 'unknown knowns' are inefficient because we have to search for and extract such latent knowledge before it can be used.

AI should have a role in capturing and recording hidden knowledge and make it explicit (via. automated knowledge discovery and management).

**Unknown unknowns (UU).** Unidentified information about a thing that has not yet been identified. We do not know enough to ask the right questions (therefore, humans are less helpful here). AI can help to detect and discover new information through exhaustive search of a system space. AlphaZero demonstrated this by discovering completely new strategies in the game of 'Go' for the first time in the 2,000-year history of the game.

We may wish to set a simple goal for AI along the lines of the following expression:

$$KK > KU + UK + UU$$

Essentially, we wish to discover, understand, encode and make accessible as much knowledge as possible to both human and AI decision-makers (aka. cognitive agents) and to do so at a rate that is faster than the world is changing (as represented by the right side of this equation).

Of course, this will never be achievable because as we act, we are increasing the right side of this equation. Nevertheless, engineering AI to continuously translate Known Unknowns, Unknown Knowns and Unknown Unknowns into Known Knowns must be a fundamental goal in pursuing a cognitive advantage. The more we can act with confidence (on Known Knowns) the more competitive we will be.

## The Relationship between Complexity Science and Data Science

To conclude this chapter, I want to briefly touch on the relationship between complexity science and data science, because whilst they are intrinsically linked, they are not synonymous.

Data science isn't enough. Data science gives us information and some knowledge. Causal analysis tells us why the data is being produced; it goes one step, two steps, three steps upstream of the data and says why that data is created in the first place. We need to move into causal analysis. And then, given the complexity of the systems we are interested in, causal science on its own does not have all the tools necessary to get upstream of the data.

Complexity science is the means for us to do that. Within the framework of the 'wisdom hierarchy' we need the tools of causal analysis to have confidence in our knowledge. And yet, even here, we need to combine knowledge in a way that we are gaining both a broad and a deep understanding of our environment.

Causal analysis can tell us why some things are happening, but – on its own – it doesn't reveal to us what may happen next, or give us the tools to explore different scenarios, to synthesise a world in which disparate knowledge is fused and presented in an intuitive and accessible way. Machine learning is a data-driven activity. Logic and reasoning are knowledge-driven activities.

This is where complexity science comes in, and it is why I put complexity science on an equal footing with AI as essential to building and maintaining a cognitive advantage. Complexity science is about studying systems and understanding unpredictable dynamic behaviour where there is circular causality, non-linear feedback, or unpredictable emergent behaviour.

Complexity science is a developing field. As we try to solve challenges in increasingly complex systems – and with accelerating AI and automation, all technological systems are increasingly complex – complexity science becomes essentially important as a scientific discipline. We need a way to manage increasing uncertainty.

Complexity science has a significant role in helping an organisation pursue a cognitive advantage; but few organisations are currently investing in it. It is still seen as a niche and somewhat nascent scientific discipline. Complexity science has traditionally been quite challenging, requiring a mathematician, physicist or biologist – that level of skill and training – to be able to do it; and usually in highly skilled, highly specialised multidisciplinary teams.

Perhaps this is part of the reason it has not seen mainstream adoption. However, Big Data and data science becoming more widely practised provides the foundation for complexity science. Everything that has enabled data science to go mainstream – cloud computing, cheaper access to more data – will also benefit complexity science.

Where complexity science steps up from data science is that it brings with it, by default, a focus on understanding systems, first and foremost. To understand a system, we recognise that we need access to data about that system. We have a hypothesis, and we need to test that hypothesis. We start from understanding the problem we are trying to solve, or the objective we are trying to achieve, and then working back to determine the data that we need.

Data science is a response to the availability of data; complexity science has a very different motivation for using data. In complexity science, data is the means to an end, it is not the end in itself.

Much of data science is application-specific, driven by specific questions an organisation wants to answer; it is a specialised function that will continue to grow in importance. Complexity science asks general questions about the world we live in and the environment an organisation exists in and uses data science to help to gain critical insights to validate, or refute, our assumptions and hypotheses.

Where previously I talked about general artificial intelligence as something considerably more than machine learning; I am now defining complexity science as general data science.

It is that generality – the ability to see the bigger picture and make lateral leaps between disconnected concepts – that sets complexity science apart. From understanding the bigger picture, we can spot emergent behaviour as it is forming. We are better equipped to anticipate how the environment might change in the future.

Once we anticipate how the environment might change we may have a preference for what we want to happen, and we can do something deliberate to make a possible event a reality or to disrupt it from happening. This is the very essence of what cognitive advantage is about, and we need complexity science, alongside tools such as AI and synthetic environments, to master this.

Where data science improves our ability to predict, complexity science improves our ability to prepare.

# Chapter 6

# Leadership and Uncertainty

*'... human action is non-linear; we need to rethink the nature of organisations and the roles of managers and leaders in them'*[30]

Ralph Stacey

The world is now more interconnected and more diverse than ever before, which means it is increasingly complex. In the modern workplace it seems that change is the only constant, and uncertainty has become the only certainty. These deceptively simple conclusions reflect changes in the context in which organisations must now operate.

As a result, all organisations are faced with levels of uncertainty and ambiguity, to the point that conventional thinking about management and leadership can only help in a limited way. This is because the underlying assumptions of conventional thinking, namely reductionism, rationalism and systems thinking, are only applicable to relatively stable and predictable situations and contexts.

However, the emerging field of complexity theory – the study of how systems interact and change over time, the subject of the previous chapter – suggests that because of the degree of interconnectedness in modern

171

organisations it is no longer possible to predict with any certainty what the future may hold.

Hence, in most organisations there will be a growing trend of greater ambiguity in the present and greater uncertainty about the future. The scale and scope of information available – often itself incomplete – is creating a sense of overload for many. As the rate and intensity of change increases, most people are struggling to make sense of their environment.

The increased complexity of our work environment necessitates a re-think of how we understand leadership and culture. The nature of leadership needs to move away from the traditional 'command and control' approach to one that is more open and holistic, that champions the central role of communities, and that is confident and purposeful in working with ambiguity and incomplete knowledge. This new form of leadership also understands the critical importance of delegating authority and decentralising decision-making.

The risk of continuing with traditional forms of leadership is that they are already producing diminishing (and possibly negative) returns. Under increasing conditions of change and uncertainty, the way leaders use knowledge to make decisions requires a re-think.

Such complexity gives rise to uncertainties: is our corporate strategy the *right* strategy? Which technology is about to go mainstream? Can we maintain our current tempo of operation? What will the world be like in twelve months' time? This creates a dilemma for leadership – how to motivate and lead a workforce when it is not always possible to provide even basic answers to the most important and pressing questions.

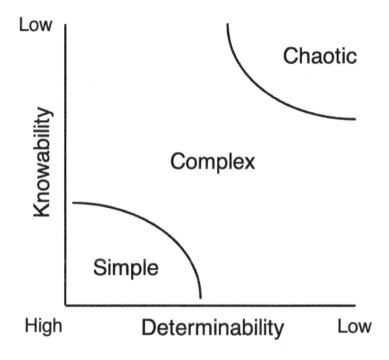

*Figure 11. Knowability (the extent to which problems and challenges can be known and understood) and Determinability (the certainty we feel about the outcome of some action) decrease as an environment becomes more complex. New leaders exhibiting new skills and behaviours are required to help guide others through such highly uncertain and ambiguous terrain. Adapted from Ralph Stacey's work.*

A new, more radical understanding of organisations in uncertain environments is emerging from the field of complexity theory. Defining an organisation as a complex network of individuals, teams and communities who work together in a self-organised way to continually make sense of their environment and to adapt in response, provides the basis for developing a complete and viable strategy. This calls for a re-definition of what it means to be a 'good leader' whilst also challenging traditional notions of where leadership and authority should reside in an organisation.

Reducing ambiguity and embracing uncertainty rest at the heart of a new leadership strategy that equips people and organisations to not just survive in these challenging times, but to flourish.

## Knowledge and Uncertainty

Broadly speaking, conventional approaches to decision making assume (i) a high level of knowledge about the present; and (ii) a reasonable certainty about the future. Such environments are assumed to reside at the bottom left of Figure 11.

Most orthodox tools and techniques have been developed for this environment. It is a world of complete information and determinism, where issues are well known and understood, and in which we are certain about the outcomes of our actions.

This does not mean that entities that exist here are simple: large scale systems can be deconstructed into small parts that may require little involvement or interaction from humans. Such projects are complicated, not complex. The distinction between the two relates to interaction and adaptation: where these exist, we are in the world of complex systems. And as we find ourselves in a more complex environment we begin to move away from certainty, to ambiguity and uncertainty.

The less we know about some issue, problem or situation, the more we can seek to improve the knowledge we have. Historically we would quite quickly reach a point at which it became too expensive or simply not possible to gain more knowledge. Now, however, with the option to use data science and AI to automate the discovery of new knowledge, those bounds can be expanded considerably.

Once we understand that organisations are made up of human beings who are continuously in dialogue with each other, and who are continuously interacting with and adapting to each other – and AI doing likewise – we can view an organisation as a complex network, with people and AI depicted as the nodes, and ideas and information flowing between them.

Such networks intrinsically deal with issues of incomplete knowledge, limited understanding, and uncertainty about the future. Humans naturally learn through interaction and adapt accordingly.

Many approaches to organisational management and leadership frame the world as if it remained in the high knowledge, high certainty quadrant. It is important to recognise that we have moved in to an 'Age of Uncertainty' and our approach to organisations must adapt accordingly. We need to be prepared to accept that the world is increasingly complex, and that uncertainty is now the norm.

The question remains: what do we do about it? And how do we position ourselves to not only survive in a seemingly perpetual state of uncertainty, but to thrive on it?

Our experience of life tells us that our environment and therefore our situation changes through time. However, classical economic theory has framed society and social systems (that is, groups of people interacting and transacting to fulfil their goals) as unchanging.

By contrast, a social system viewed as a complex network is one that operates in patterns of behaviours, but also that learns and adapts in unpredictable ways over time. This distinction is profoundly important for understanding how organisations should be led, governed, and managed.

In many organisations, the response is for a senior leadership team to try to make sense of their environment more frequently, in order to have a robust confidence in their subsequent analysis and plans, and to communicate their findings rapidly to an international workforce.

How likely is it that the workforce in such an organisation will be able to effect the necessary changes quickly enough that those changes remain a valid response to a changing environment? It is unlikely to be a success and even more unlikely to be sustainable over time, leading to a 'change fatigued' workforce.

Unwieldy and unsustainable as this scenario may be, most organisations continue to try and operate in just such a way. Failure won't be immediate, but unless these organisations change their approach, they will gradually succumb to an environment they can no longer make sense of. Such is the risk for those leaders who continue to view organisations as deterministic, predictable systems that can be aligned to fit with their environment through top-down executive action.

Any system is most sustainable when it has the right balance of efficiency and resilience. If a system is insufficiently efficient it is likely to fail – it will not be viable. If a system is insufficiently resilient – and unable to adapt as the wider environment changes – it will also fail.

The optimal zone is where the system is both sufficiently efficient and sufficiently resilient – which I introduced in Chapter 3 as the *window of viability*.

Highly efficient systems typically have too little interconnectivity and/or too little diversity. They act as a closed system that is attempting to 'keep the world at bay'. This type of organisation will be brittle and will be prone to shocks that it is poorly equipped to adapt to.

Equivalently, systems that are highly resilient will be insufficiently efficient – they will be prone to extinction as their consumption outstrips their supply and they are unable to generate enough valued work or to produce the results that keep their supply – money and resources – topped up. An important aspect of understanding where change may be occurring in an environment is the concept of emergence, as discussed in Chapter 5.

Within the context of an organisation, emergence is the simple idea that a sufficiently complex system will learn over time and that this learning will yield new and unexpected behaviours.

How often has it been the case that a well-developed strategy and a highly motivated workforce still meets with failure? Why it is that market leaders sometimes see their market dominance disappear almost overnight? The most likely answer is that they are operating in a complex environment that is evolving faster than they can keep up.

Changes in the environment are evidence of emergent behaviour within the system the organisation is operating in. As you would expect, emergence may represent a threat or an opportunity. The skill is in spotting new patterns of behaviour as they begin to emerge, making sense of what that new pattern of behaviour means – is it a friend or foe? – and attaching some meaning to it – 'we have a great opportunity here' or 'RUN!'.

The viability of an organisation is a function of its ability to perform pattern recognition, make sense of emergent behaviour within its environment, and respond swiftly.

The ability to not just name the beast but to also articulate its features and describe its behaviour needs to become embedded as a core competency for an organisation seeking to operate consistently in the window of viability – but change is happening around us all the time, so how is it possible for leaders to gain mastery of pattern recognition?

The answer is they don't – at least – they don't do it alone. They share the burden with other people, and they use AI.

## Re-Thinking Leadership

Every person in an organisation is in contact with others and with their environment – whether that is their physical surroundings, their relationships, or simply their knowledge of what is going on. As such, everyone has the potential to spot patterns which may be indicative of change emerging. In that sense, anyone can lead through uncertain terrain, by reducing ambiguity and making sense of what is happening. Such a concept – where everyone sees themselves as a leader – can be thought of as a 'leaderful' organisation.

Whether we realise it or not, humans are highly effective at pattern recognition. It is intrinsic to our psychological and neurological development. And we do it all the time. In meetings or discussions with colleagues we are often seeking solutions to problems. Sometimes these are problems we have anticipated. Oftentimes they are not. We tend to follow a loosely defined process that correlates to Diagnose → Cure. This works effectively for well-bounded and well understood problems, where we have a high degree of knowledge and certainty about likely outcomes.

But what about the hidden aspects of organisational life? Those things that 'we don't know we don't know' or where we 'can't quite put our finger' on the problem. These are the Unknown Unknowns and Unknown Knowns that we discussed in the previous chapter. How many times have we read or heard a highly successful businessperson talk about 'going with their gut instinct'? This is just intuition waiting for intellect to catch up – but there is risk if it takes too long for intellect to do that.

Elevating the importance of exploring our intuition with others is valuable for an organisation aiming to remain within the window of viability.

Throughout this book I have made these, or similar, points. I have also outlined how AI can help us explore our intuition, discover new knowledge and crystallise it into informed action. We ask the questions; AI can help with the answers. AI may even suggest the questions we should be asking.

There are five themes to understanding what this means for a new form of leadership:

1. 'Sense-making' and 'Meaning-making'
2. Levels of work
3. Re-thinking authority and accountability
4. Enabling creativity
5. Values and behaviours

Investing time in exploring intuitive insight needs to become a common way of working. Senior leaders need to elevate the importance of making sense of possible changes in the environment in a proactive and embracing way, across the breadth and depth of an organisation. As such, the culture needs to enable creativity – both individually and collectively, both artificial and human – as a critical activity that keeps an organisation in the window of viability.

And finally, in organisations that reside in more conventional cultures, their formal leaders need to think anew about values and behaviours. Fostering a work environment that enables and encourages greater sharing and delegation of responsibility for setting vision and strategy. This will require full engagement of the workforce themselves. Meaningful values and behaviours should come from the workforce and new leaders can facilitate that dialogue.

## Sense-Making and Meaning-Making

In the context of ambiguity and uncertainty it is vital that teams and leaders understand how to bring to bear the full potential of themselves and other teams. This means genuinely understanding the vitality, creative potential and emergent properties of human conversation and deliberately deploying it as an asset for high performance. This process is called sense-making and meaning-making (and we undertake these activities as we cycle through the Perception-Action loops from Chapter 3).

If technology and social systems are constantly evolving, and we are therefore in a perpetual state of change, then perhaps the most important role we have as leaders is to continuously make sense of the environment in which we are operating. We need sense-making skills.

We can unpack this term to help us understand it better. Sense-making can be about identifying new and emerging themes that are influencing an organisation, e.g., customers may have started to ask unexpected questions and to state new needs. An individual, a team, or a community needs to be able to make sense of these changes.

A second example is that tensions may arise within these entities which require some form of resolution. Ideally such tensions will be identified and resolved before they rupture and cause damage.

Third, unsustainable practices might emerge that render a team or community non-viable over time, for example, they are spending too much effort on one activity (ensuring that they are compliant with regulations) at the expense of a separate and more valued activity (giving the customer what they need).

The second and third examples here both require making sense of the problem in an accurate way, in order to move toward resolution. There are many ways in which sense-making can be achieved. Typically, a team or community needs to have good communication channels in place in order to understand what is going on within the team/community and its wider terrain of work, and individuals need to cultivate good pattern-recognition skills to make sense of it all.

The role of the leader here is one of facilitation – helping people to better understand the nature of what they are doing both individually and as a team. This then helps them to continue to experience their work in a meaningful way.

To use a well-worn, probably apocryphal, example, when a floor sweeper who worked for a global logistics company was asked what their job was, they answered, 'Making sure people get their parcels delivered on time'. Their job – keeping factory and office workspaces clean and tidy – had only a distant effect on their organisation's ability to fulfil its purpose; but that is not really the point. However, it came about, this person had attached real meaning to their work, and it gave them a sense of motivation and commitment.

It is important that a leader promote dialogue with individuals in the team to help them understand their purpose. This process is called meaning-making and the leader works with individuals and teams to interpret broader themes and trends, identified in the process of sense-making, so that they can make sense and attach meaning to changes in the environment. From this they can then collectively understand what response may be required and why.

It is also important to note that this activity – of sense-making and meaning-making – reduces the need for senior leaders to interpret changes and attach meaning on behalf of the workforce. Thus, making sense of the environment and adapting through effective responses can be done on a localised basis with little (if any) direction or oversight from senior management.

This is a radical step, as it decouples the organisation's ability to respond to its environment from the limitations of corporate planning and executive action. With the advent of AI to augment human abilities, at all levels of an organisation, this may well herald a transition to a truly decentralised organisation.

There are tools available which can facilitate sense-making and meaning-making through a process of mapping conversations, which make it much easier for everyone to become aware of emerging themes. This can create a powerful and creative dynamic between communities, team members and leaders.

Related to sense-making and meaning-making is the process of *cognitive framing*. Often, as situations evolve, there can be several interpretations (or framings) of what is happening. The more complex the environment, the more susceptible it will be to multiple frames of reference. A leader would typically seek to make sense of these multiple interpretations through dialogue with others and to attach meaning as appropriate.

Sense-making and meaning-making are two sides of the same coin; or, put more technically, they constitute a dialectic, and facilitating this is a critical skill of leadership under conditions of uncertainty and ambiguity.

These sense-making activities need leaders, but not necessarily formal ones.

Guiding a group of people through an exploratory and dynamic discussion to reduce ambiguity and bring forth new understanding requires a capability to handle complex information and a natural aptitude for relationships. These two skills are not often found together, and as the complexity of a situation increases, the more crucial they become.

## Levels of Work

Highly capable individuals who are emotionally aware and well connected exist within every organisation at every level. Such individuals may have naturally gravitated to a role in their community in which they are valued and respected and listened to, because they somehow seem to be able to make sense of what is happening. These are new types of leaders operating within the *leaderful* organisation. Tapping into this potential requires the formal leaders of an organisation to legitimise such community leader roles.

Taking the perspective of an organisation as a complex network might lead us to assume that it is flat and non-hierarchical. In fact, research has emphasised that complex networks involve hierarchy. This is vital for organisations to understand, especially those operating nationally and internationally, because their work will involve higher levels of complexity.

Such work has been pioneered by Elliot Jaques who emphasised that complexity occurs at discrete levels in an organisation and thus requires pattern recognition of varying depth as we move between those levels.

Jaques analysed tens of thousands of positions – including the CEOs - of top US companies to understand the work that was required of them and how they were processing information. He wanted to know - what made them successful? From this research he developed a system of seven levels of work (called Stratified Systems Theory), with each requiring increasing abilities to process increasingly complex (ambiguous, uncertain, incomplete, rapidly changing) information. Based on his empirical research he identified that each person has an innate ability which corresponds to a level on that scale.

Understanding levels of work has important implications for leadership. There is a key relationship between work levels and sense-making and meaning-making. We can think of these levels as representing degrees of complexity, requiring different pattern- recognition (sense-making) skills at different levels.

For example, Level 1 roles involve concrete work e.g., people doing repetitive work that does not require particularly complex pattern recognition skills. Level 2 roles will require basic pattern recognition skills, which allow for the leadership of Level 1 roles. Similarly, Level 3 roles require deeper pattern recognition than Level 2: leaders at this level will help provide context (sense-making) to those at Level 2. There are parallels here with the *wisdom hierarchy* that I described in Chapter 3.

AI may help automate Level 1 and 2 work whilst augmenting humans who are performing Level 3–5 work. Level 3 is about supervising other people to help them do their jobs; levels 4 and 5 are about being able to think strategically, to understand what is going on outside the organisation, in society, what competitors are doing, and interpret what it means for the organisation; levels 6 and 7 are the people who can foresee the future and know how to intervene in their present-day environment to build the foundations for the future they have a vision of.

His work can be somewhat contentious if misinterpreted. It is an interesting concept that as leaders we benefit from considering; and then there is the risk of unintended consequences, that we may end up artificially segregating our workforce. If used sensibly, however, it is a tool that could help people understand how they can find work that is best suited to them, based on their ability – and their desire – to do work that empathises (or equally valid, de-empathises) processing of complex information.

The key is that these levels of complex information processing should be presented as a tool to help people, to act as a career compass, rather than being a dictate set from the top. It will become clearer as we explain it.

Jaques saw all levels with the CEOs he interviewed. It shocked people that he said some of the CEOs he interviewed were operating at level 1 and 2; but that is not a great surprise given the historical tendency to recruit and promote staff who 'fit-the-mould'. Most CEOs, Jaques said, are at level 3. They are good supervisors and can get good productivity out of their workforce. In terms of the window of viability, and total shareholder return – bearing in mind this research was in the 80s – his research showed that CEOs tended to be those who are good at cutting costs and getting their people to deliver maximum output. He saw less evidence of strategy-making or foresighted, insightful perception of what was really going on.

He came up with some recommendations based on his research. One of them was that he didn't think total shareholder return is going to go away, nor the appetite of a board of directors and of shareholders to look to their CEO to be the leader in terms of efficiency and profitability; however, Jaques says, therein lies a big risk, because that way of operating leads to lack of diversity. It neglects situational awareness, keeping in touch with what competitors are doing, with how things are changing, where there might be new profit-making opportunities. He said it was important that the CEOs build a team around themselves with level 4, 5, 6 and 7 capabilities – although interestingly he said that level 7 individuals probably would not work within a company structure, because companies are too narrow and short-term focused for the level 7 thinker.

An ability to handle complex, often incomplete information and the subsequent uncertainty that this creates is now an essential skill. We can no longer just shrug our shoulders and say we can't move forward. We need to come up with ideas, generate hypotheses, do experiments and find out what we can do to give a greater sense of meaning to our environment. This is a creative process.

Moving up these levels, we see more of that ability to handle information, make sense of it, assimilate it, comprehend it, perceive what it might mean, possibly see one or two or three ways to validate the accuracy of that perception, then also have the foresight – like chess moves – to think three or four or five steps ahead of where we are.

Jaques's work occurred before AI started to become mainstream. AI, in most cases, could perform the first three levels – not that we would use AI to supervise humans, but to automate the management of other AI, e.g., robots on a manufacturing line, or recommender software on Amazon or Netflix.

Previously we talked about data, information, knowledge and wisdom as the hierarchical levels of cognition. Jaques's view is a different way of thinking about the cognitive capacity of our organisation. Not that we will do away with humans completely at levels 1-3, because there will still be humans who are managing AI or managing things that can't be done automatically by robots and AI; but in terms of workforce strategy, in terms of the trajectory we want our organisation to go on, in terms of people, their skills and attitudes and roles, their job design, Jaques' levels of complex information processing is a useful tool to make sense of those things.

It also affects recruitment policy, because as AI is doing more of the low-level tasks, we might want to recruit more creative people, more people from the humanities, whose training is more directed towards creativity than is typical in technical fields. We will also want to recruit people who can operate at those higher levels of work.

He went on to develop a methodology to assess complex information processing ability via a series of interviews, each one an hour or two, conducted by an interviewer trained in how to ask questions and interpret answers to track thought processes. These levels of complex information processing have multiple uses in the cognitive enterprise, specifically when designing our collective artificial and human intellect workforce: what kind of jobs will suit which people, what kind of jobs are better done by machines. It also gives us a way to evaluate and select the best type of people to lead the organisation moving forward. If you are looking for sagacious leaders, people who have deep insight and are also willing to accept uncertainty, these will probably be level 4, 5, 6 and 7 – not level 3.

His work may help people be honest with themselves, to think about what type of role they may be best suited to. Talking to my clients and fellow consultants we have all observed the effect that a poor person-job fit has on both the individual and the organisation. Oftentimes this is because people are operating at a level above where they should be, people who have been promoted – because they are awesome supervisors – into a C-suite position.

Yet, leadership at that level requires a different mindset and attitude: it is about strategy, persuasion and accepting ambiguity. They fundamentally struggle, because they have been rewarded based on level 3 behaviour, but that behaviour is not what is needed here. They may have a latent level 4/5 capability, and coaching may help them to make the adjustment; but some people just cannot handle the uncertainty and flood of information that occurs at a strategic level.

We need to discover ways to reward and recognise our people for being awesome at what they are doing. If we link reward and recognition only to job titles, then we are at risk of losing the brains and talent that have made the organisation a success in the first place.

The skills that led to success in that bygone age are not what is needed now; and the ways we assessed suitability for leadership positions are also out of date. We need new criteria to guide the search. Thinking about leadership in terms of complex information processing capabilities may help in devising new talent and workforce strategies.

Figure 12 illustrates the first five levels of work and how they relate to work that is done at increasing degrees of complexity. For example, work of low complexity (that is, where we have high level of knowledge and high level of certainty about the work we are doing) is classed as being at Level 1. By comparison, under conditions of significant uncertainty (levels 3, 4 and 5) the nature of the work itself is more complex and demanding and typically involves considerable dialogue and engagement across a broad range of stakeholders. There is a high degree of uncertainty over what the outcome might be.

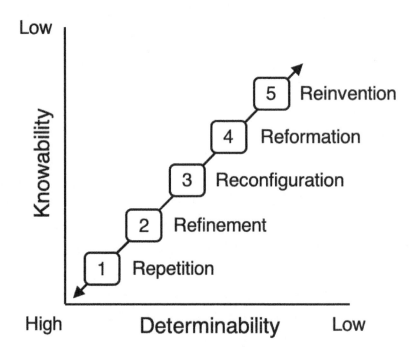

*Figure 12. Levels of Work. Integrating Jaques's research on human capability and levels of work into Stacey's knowability/determinability. The five levels shown indicate the general nature of the work undertaken at varying degrees of complexity, with Level 1 being the most deterministic and simple and level 5 the most complex and uncertain.*

Jaques emphasised that people vary in their ability to lead and manage at these different levels. Different levels are suited to different people. When there is a mismatch, leadership and management are likely to be sub-optimal.

He also developed techniques for appreciating individuals' suitability for different levels of work. There are firms that specialise in helping organisations make use of these techniques, either as part of evaluating potential senior recruits or as part of developing senior leaders.

As we move into higher levels, the more abstract – and deeper – the requirement for pattern recognition becomes. Those operating at Level 5 will have to make sense of very deep trends that relate to their domain. This will require a considerable understanding of pertinent social and technological trends, as well as a general grasp of their immediate surroundings.

A typical example would be a leader looking to identify similarities and differences in values between Generations W, X, and Y, in their workforce, and what this means for the organisation. Whilst AI excels at pattern recognition in general, within this context I am referring to the ability to perceive recurring behaviours in complex and dynamic environments.

Leaders at this level would help to transform the organisation (facilitate adaptation and catalyse change) in relevant ways, for example, to offer employment that is attractive to all generations, and to help leadership at lower levels to understand what these inter-generational shifts mean for them. In this sense, the leader is reinventing the meaning that people can attach to their career with the subsequent benefit of improving their motivation and contribution.

It should be emphasised that while 'hierarchy' is a word used in the technical literature, this does not mean that organisations ought to be run with a traditional, hierarchical command and control structure. Here, hierarchy merely recognises that complex networks can and do exhibit discrete layers of operation, and this is true of work within organisations. This also has implications for authority and accountability.

Whilst I have focused here on leadership and people there is a significant role for AI in operating at each of Jaques's *levels of work* and in helping humans do so too (and this is an active area of research for the author).

## Re-Thinking Accountability and Authority

It remains a surprise to realise that in most areas of industry, dominant management practice still portrays the organisation like a machine, and employees like automatons. In such approaches, authority and accountability are typically weighted toward the top of the organisation: lower levels are largely responsible for carrying out decisions made at the top, which are cascaded downwards by managers.

A complexity approach leads us to think of organisations in a materially different way. In effect, we need to think of organisations as consisting of multiple overlapping communities. In developing an appropriate culture one objective is to nest the requisite authority and accountability with appropriate communities. These responsibilities will include the community's role in the organisation and the understanding of how each community relates to others and what is expected and required of each.

Each community might have within it multiple sub-communities that have particular purposes within the wider community. For example, a software engineering community might have groups dedicated to specific types of work, with a formal core leadership team and informal community leaders.

The purpose of both the formal and informal leadership is to make sense of the wider community and the challenges it faces, and to enable all parts of that community in appropriate ways.

In the context of communities, leadership becomes one of selecting the right staff and enabling the constituents of the community. In terms of levels of work, communities ought to be led by people with the appropriate pattern-recognition skills to facilitate sense-making and meaning-making. Larger and more complex communities, made up of smaller, nested communities, will require leadership at ever higher levels of capability. These constructs – of nested and overlapping communities – can be thought of as constellations of communities.

As a constellation of communities, the levels of work that need to be performed, the authority to make decisions, and the responsibility and accountability concerning the outcome of those decisions all need to be correctly calibrated and allocated within the organisation. For top-heavy organisations, in which most authority resides with senior managers, this typically requires a process of devolution.

If this is done appropriately, a key role of senior leaders and managers is to provide the conditions that enable this devolution of power, and which enable people and communities to exercise their authority appropriately in meeting their responsibilities.

The goal of policy regarding authority and accountability should be to maximise the freedoms of communities sufficient to enable them to take ownership of their own purpose and their own ways of organising themselves to fulfil such a purpose.

Such self-organising communities are a critical concept to understand, as they are one of the most effective solutions for achieving high performance in complex and uncertain environments.

## Unlocking Creativity

Creativity is fundamental to an organisation's ability to keep within its window of viability. First, it helps organisations to become more efficient and/or more resilient. Second, creativity facilitates adaptation as the environment changes. Without creativity an organisation risks remaining in a static state, lacking the ability to respond to change.

In an increasingly complex and demanding environment it can oftentimes feel that the perpetual mood in an organisation is one of firefighting, where the capacity for thinking, exploring, inventing, and being innovative tends to get suppressed under the remorseless load of 'more urgent' work that needs to be done. This is a deeply risky situation. The organisation is likely to be expending too much effort on delivery at the expense of a diversity of ideas and solutions.

Complexity theory has a few useful things to say about creativity.

First, it is impossible to predict how people will be creative and therefore we cannot really plan for it – if future creativity were known beforehand, it would not be novel, so it would not be creative.

Second, creativity is enabled by diversity. Consider an extreme case in which the executive team of a company consists of carbon copies of the CEO: such a team is unlikely to be creative because it is homogenous – as far as creativity is concerned, the team may as well contain one person. In human systems, creativity typically arises from the interaction of people with sufficiently diverse views, opinions, and perspectives.

Third, creativity must be enabled in part through resource being available as appropriate. This latter point ties in with resilience: the focus of an organisation should not be efficiency alone – in a constantly evolving world, resilience must be respected.

What is the role for leadership in enabling and encouraging creativity?

The first is to select teams to reflect a diverse and appropriate portfolio of education, skills and experience, and ensure individuals also have good interpersonal skills to allow them to cope with different points of view. These differences may be elevated to conflict of opinion and ideas, which means good communication and people-handling skills become essential.

The second aspect is for leaders to facilitate conversation between team members in a way that might involve tension, but which also offers the possibility of creative break-through. Innovation is not guaranteed, but the role of the leader in this scenario is to provide the conditions for creativity. For example, a leader may observe that the team is polarised around a particular solution. In such a case the team's thinking is probably too tightly integrated.

We may wish to inject one or more contentious or challenging ideas that differ significantly from the dominant view. This action – of introducing different ideas and viewpoints – promotes differentiated thinking within the team. We are attempting to maximise the creative potential of the group.

As ideas and opinions become more varied and diverse, we then have the equally important task of bringing into focus common patterns emerging in the conversation. This integration of ideas back into a form that the team may agree on helps everyone make sense and attach meaning to the subject matter.

Unsurprisingly, the process of managing creativity is little different from that of keeping an organisation in the window of viability. Too little difference of opinion can lead to stagnation; too much difference of opinion can lead to chaos. And, as such, those same leadership skills of pattern recognition, sense-making, and meaning-making are just as relevant in unlocking the full creative potential of individuals, teams and communities across the organisation.

## Values and Behaviours

Orthodox approaches to leadership typically emphasise two different types of behaviours required of us – leadership through demonstrating human values, and the exercise of particular characteristics. Good work has been done in both domains over many years and some of it links well with the above five themes of leadership.

Traditional approaches to leadership typically empathise particular values, including being respectful, inclusivity, collaboration, sensitivity, listening, sharing (not hoarding) information, promoting well-being, and so on.

Equivalently, behavioural characteristics are also traditionally associated with leadership. These typically include agility and resilience, developing relationships, engagement with and within the team, management of talent, and encouraging collaboration.

What is often missing from such approaches to leadership is the appreciation of why these traits are important. Often, they are presented as statements of fact, without substantiation. Commonly, this is because many of them have emerged through experience. The lens of complex networks is a robust and legitimate cognitive framework and gives us a useful perspective on why particular traits might be worthwhile.

The point to emphasise here is that the purpose of exercising particular values and behavioural characteristics is to support the previous five themes. In the language of mathematics, values are endogenous: an innate and learned response to pursuing the explicit and implicit aims of the organisation.

Moreover, when we take a complex networks view of organisations it becomes clear that we must take care in prescribing a particular set of values or behavioural characteristics.

There are two broad reasons for this: idiosyncrasies and context. Any organisation will have its own operational environment, with its own unique circumstances, which means the types of values consistent with one organisation operating in the window of viability will be different to those of another organisation.

Perhaps more importantly, within organisations, context matters. Extreme care must be taken to prescribe a list of 'value-rules', which must be followed in each circumstance because in some circumstances, a value-rule may be inappropriate.

Traditional approaches emphasise exogenous facts, the 'we should use these values because they are best practice' type of thinking. This imposition of values from outside of an organisation's own communities will lack legitimacy and, as such, is highly likely to fail.

This point is important not only for appreciating what values and characteristics are best suited to certain contexts; it also highlights the motivation for their adoption. And motivation matters when it comes to influencing behaviour.

These points aside, the responsibility for good *values leadership* is greater with those who are more visible in, and have a bigger influence on, organisations.

Network theory, which is a part of the study of complex networks, suggests that networks can include agents with multiple nodes and strong influences on the whole network.

We can call these 'super-influencers'. This means that senior managers, who are known throughout an organisation, will normally be leaders by default (good or bad) because their behaviour will be known by many – directly, and indirectly, through informal channels of communication (including gossip).

There are also 'multipliers', as identified by Liz Wiseman: those who freely and effectively pass on wisdom to others and, in the process, help them make better decisions. Her idea, that if we help others be smarter then collectively we will achieve more, calls for the culling of the information is power mindset that, it grieves me to say, I still see significant evidence of.

To continue with the metaphor of a workforce as a complex network, if I were to show you a real-time graphic that represented the flow of knowledge across your workforce, and if green nodes and links represented free flowing knowledge and red a poor flow of knowledge, you would – quite likely – want to fix those red nodes and links.

Yet, because we don't use data in this way, we don't challenge the behaviour that the data is telling us exists. The effect of what Charles Handy calls 'negative power' – that is, people enacting a form of passive aggression to exert influence, such as withholding critical knowledge that they know will help a colleague make a better decision – ultimately leads to poor overall performance. Negative power may be invisible to us, for now, but as we begin to use data to gain an accurate depiction of our organisation, such behaviours are likely to dissipate – if the will is there to act on such insight.

It is also important to appreciate that while organisations typically have formal organisational structures, they also contain vibrant informal networks of relationships and communication. These 'shadow networks' are often much more important in terms of values and culture than the organisation's official reporting structure. In complex social networks everybody contributes to values and culture. Nobody sits in isolation from everybody else. In complex social networks, people co-create values – everybody has some power in this regard, which means everybody has a duty to exercise that power responsibly. So, everybody is involved with values leadership.

The study of complex networks provides a framework to help us make sense of complex issues. It is a framework that resonates with the increased complexity of the world in which we now live, and it helps us to better understand the nature of good leadership in new circumstances.

Most organisations will recognise the importance of undertaking activities to define values and behaviours. However, most also tend to over-emphasise the importance of this. It is a necessary but not sufficient response to developing an effective leadership and culture strategy. Indeed, we have suggested that values and behaviours should be calibrated in response to the other four themes that we have outlined.

Building and maintaining a cognitive advantage is fundamentally dependent on every person in an organisation – from the senior leadership to the general worker – achieving their full potential.

The starting point for understanding this is to appreciate that every person has innate abilities that means they may be better suited to certain types of cognitive work than others. In addition, the autonomy of people and teams is key to the organisation's ability to perceive, understand and act on changes in the environment.

# Chapter 7

# Shaping the Environment

*'.. each cyclops had a single eye because the other was traded to the Gods for the ability to see into the future. However, they were tricked and the only vision they had was of the day they would die. Theirs was the unending torture of being forewarned and yet having no ability to do anything about it.* '[31]

An interpretation of a Greek Myth

Now, this quote may be too melodramatic for a book about AI, and yet the underlying concept – an inability to act to avoid an undesirable future – is important. We can have fantastic insights to how the world is changing, how technology is changing, and how we are changing, but without the ability to act we are no different from the cyclops.

We need to explore what it means to act and formulate strategies where humans are attempting to make sense of an environment. Important fields of science such as psychology and behavioural science are relevant here. We should also not overlook the importance of having a highly effective feedback loop between acting and accurately sensing the effect that such action has had.

## Changing People's Behaviours

Nudge Theory is a concept that was introduced by Richard Thaler (an economist) and Cass Sunstein (a legal scholar) within the field of behavioural science that focused on understanding how people think, make decisions and behave. Their argument was that as we gain a deeper understanding into these factors, we can devise small interventions, in either the physical domain or information domain, to influence a change in people's behaviours.

An infamous example of a successful 'nudge' is to encourage men to be more accurate, shall we say, when using a public toilet, by placing an image of a house fly at a preferred point on the urinal. To understand how nudge theory works, we need to understand a little more about psychology.

In 1943, the American psychologist Abraham Maslow published a seminal paper, 'A Theory of Human Motivation' in which he described his famous hierarchy of needs (see Figure 13). Maslow's theory was simple: we need to satisfy the conditions at a lower level of this pyramid before we can move to satisfy the conditions at a higher level. You cannot achieve 'self-actualisation' if you are hungry, under threat, or ill, is how the theory goes.

Nowadays, there is a general acceptance that we are not as rigid as this suggests and, if anything, the satisfaction of our needs is dynamic and sometimes contradictory. For example, when I used to run ultramarathons (I may have one more in me at some point), I was constantly hungry, exhausted, dehydrated and at times at real risk of hypothermia or heat stroke; yet I had never felt more alive and happier. In the pursuit of higher level needs we can temporarily forsake our lower-level needs.

Does this make Maslow's hierarchy out-dated and less relevant? No. It remains a useful starting point in thinking about why we behave the way we do. It provides a window for the layman, or the non-professional, into human psychology. It is often a sufficient tool for those seeking to influence our behaviours – politicians, marketeers, tabloid journalists – to identify ways to either convince us that a condition has been satisfied, or conversely, to convince us that a previously satisfied condition is now in jeopardy. A recent and stark reminder of this was the blunt tactics used during the UK's 2017 EU referendum, where both the Leave and the Remain campaigns, resorted to fear tactics: 'If you don't leave the EU your jobs will be taken by immigrants'; 'If we leave the EU then our economy will collapse leading to mass unemployment'.

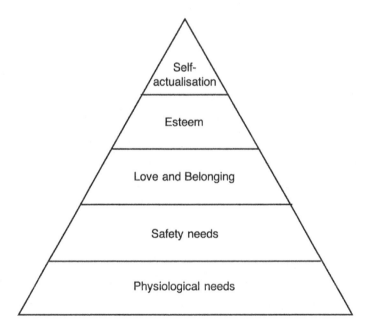

*Figure 13. Maslow's Hierarchy of Needs provides an intuitive and simple way to understand basic human desires.*

Marketing professionals seek to convince us that their product will satisfy an unmet need, even if we are currently happy and satisfied. The marketeer wants to convince us that our prestige will be heightened by purchasing their aftershave, or their skincare products, or their clothes.

This manipulation of what we believe, and therefore how we act, is as old as history. The main difference now, of course, is that the sophistication of these interventions in a fast, digital and constantly online world will become far more powerful and prevalent in influencing our thinking. There will also be a greater number of these micro-interventions.

Now, as individuals, we are on a trajectory leading to hyper-consumerism. It may feel that we are already at that point, but we are not. Personalised adverts that connect with us on an emotional level are the holy grail. A large part of the valuation of companies like Facebook is the insight and the precision with which an advert can be targeted to appear in a person's news feed at just the right time.

Maslow's hierarchy is a simple, but highly effective, window into some of the buttons that can be pushed to get us to do what other people want us to do. However, it does not explain what causes us to change our behaviours.

I have been a practising management consultant for over a decade and, prior to that, another decade as a senior leader in start-up companies and multinationals. It has been my job for over 20 years to change organisations. I have been educated in dozens of different behavioural models (I still use a few) and I can tell you this – understanding behavioural change boils down to one question: what is in it for me? If someone does not value the result of what you are asking them to do, then – apart from coercion or a threat of violence, both unethical and borderline illegal – they are very unlikely to invest the time and effort required to change.

A good strategy for effecting behavioural change, whether in an employee, a customer, a citizen, a competitor, or an adversary – is to get them to care about something that you care about. Once they care about something, then make it easy for them to take the first step towards changing their behaviour in the direction you want them to. Let me introduce you to a simple tool: the ADKAR model.

## The ADKAR Model

The ADKAR model was developed by the Prosci® consortium as a result of their research into successful business change initiatives across 236 organisations worldwide. They benchmarked and analysed each of these organisations and distilled their findings into a business change methodology and some analytical tools.

One of those tools is the ADKAR model, an acronym for: Awareness, Desire, Knowledge, Ability, and Reinforcement. These are somewhat self-evident but let's briefly describe them.

**Awareness.** How much does the person know about the change that you are advocating? Are they receiving relevant information? How do you make them aware?

**Desire.** How much do they care about the change? How much does the change align to their existing beliefs about the world? How might you change those beliefs?

**Knowledge.** How much do they understand the change? Can they make sense of the change you are proposing? Are they attaching meaning to the change? Do they understand what it might mean for them?

**Ability.** Can they engage with the change? Do they have the time and the means to do so? If they want the change, is it clear what the next step should be? Do they have enough understanding, and the means, to adopt the behaviour you wish them to?

**Reinforcement.** What is in it for them? Has this been articulated? What do they stand to gain by engaging with the change? What do they stand to lose by not engaging with the change?

Informally, when looking at an individual or a group, you simply assign some score to each of these factors (e.g., 1 to 5, or High/Medium/Low). Overall, the ADKAR score gives you an indication of how ready someone is to change their behaviour towards that which you are advocating. From that score you can then design interventions.

In a similar vein to Maslow's hierarchy of needs, the theory is that by increasing people's level in each of these categories, then you are progressing them towards satisfying that critical condition: 'I care about this' which is arrived at from satisfactorily answering the question 'What's in it for me?'.

The theory goes that a number of interventions can be made to increase someone's awareness of something (an advert, an email, a recommendation from a friend), or increase their knowledge about something (a training course, a book, a podcast), or equip them with the ability to engage with such interventions (we are busy people, how do we help them find the time to engage with these interventions?) and give them a positive reason to do so by reinforcing why something is a good idea. The most elusive is changing someone's desire, as it is a deeply rooted emotion.

Some readers may have been put off by my claim that people only change when they can satisfy the question, 'What's In It For Me?' (WIIFM). Now, for some people, WIIFM could be as simple as a financial reward. For other people, it could be something more altruistic, i.e., wanting to help someone else.

The point is that WIIFM is based on what you believe and, more profoundly, what you believe about yourself and who you believe you are. Beliefs are not static; they change over time as we learn from experiencing the world we live in. It is, therefore, important to understand how someone ticks, as their current behaviour reflects their current beliefs.

Changing people's beliefs about something can be easy ('after reading that product review on Amazon, I'm not going to buy that product anymore'), or it can be hard ('the UK is better off out of the European Union'). Desire comes from believing in something. The other elements of the ADKAR model: awareness, knowledge, ability, reinforcement are the levers to try and change someone's beliefs. How we pull on those levers may induce a large effect ('Save our NHS') or a small effect ('Try this free perfume sample'). Both effects are equally useful.

This is Marketing 101. However, the big transformation that is coming is that the evaluation of readiness, the devising of interventions and the delivery of those interventions will be increasingly done by AI at a scale and at a speed that will be incomprehensible to humans. Indeed, in Jeff Orlowski's highly insightful movie 'A Social Dilemma', we are told a compelling story that persuasion technology as used by Facebook and other tech companies is already very much with us.

Humans are less involved in deciding what other humans will read or see as AI automates the implementation of effects in the information domain to induce behavioural changes in humans through micro-interventions ('nudges'). Marketing and Advertising technology, or MarTech and AdTech as they are known, are the driving force of this transformation.

There are an almost limitless number of tactics for nudging people's behaviours. I recently saw an infographic that illustrated some of the 'levers' that behavioural scientists use to nudge people towards a desired behaviour. The infographic identified 43 'levers' spread across seven categories: Incentives, Cognitive Dissonance, Emotion, Framing, Loss Aversion, Social and Willpower. Nudge tactics can look to pull more than one lever at any time. If we were to conservatively estimate that an average nudge tactic uses two levers, then this constitutes 903 combinations to influence our behaviour.

Now even the world's best marketeers or behavioural scientists are going to get through only a fraction of those combinations during an information campaign. But an AI could routinely and simultaneously experiment in the real world with all such combinations. As the sophistication of an information campaign increases – let's say that a marketeer is now using combinations of three levers (12,341 possible combinations) or even four levers (123,410 possible combinations) - the use of humans becomes nonsensical.

Only algorithms and AI can cope with the volume and speed required for modern, digitally-enabled information campaigns.

## The Physical Domain and the Information Domain

There are two domains in which we can act: we directly act in the physical domain and indirectly act in the information domain (as illustrated in Figure 14).

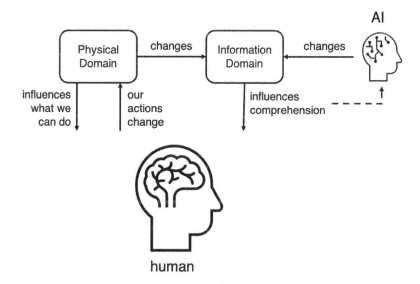

*Figure 14. Illustration of the two domains – physical and information – that humans and AI influence. Humans and AI are distinct in that humans can only influence the information domain via. the physical domain. AI can potentially access both domains directly although its interface to the physical domain is currently crude.*

The physical domain consists of things that exist in the real world:

infrastructure, products, machinery, computers, computer peripherals, smartphones, virtual reality headsets, buildings, structures and so on.

The information domain consists of data, information, knowledge. The transmission of information occurs in the physical world. The processing of information occurs in the physical world too: computers, our brain. Things that exist, or that happen, in the real world convey information.

They are complementary domains that are inextricably linked.

The action we take in one space can influence the other: creating the iPhone (a physical product) fundamentally re-shaped the information domain (digital music) as will the introduction of new technologies such as 5G and the Internet of Things, which will expand the information domain. At a more basic level, humans influence the information domain by acting in the physical domain e.g., using a computer to search the internet, write a book, create and upload a YouTube video.

Whilst our physical domain can change through our actions, it is the information domain that our cognitive functions operate in. Therefore, it is the information domain that we need to look to, to shape people's beliefs and behaviours. Humans process information before they decide to act in the physical domain. Therefore, by shaping the information domain we are influencing people's beliefs and understanding of their world. From that comprehension, humans act in the physical domain.

However, acting in the physical domain does not directly influence people's actions; its effect is indirect, via the information domain. Therefore, in devising strategies and plans to act in the physical domain, the sagacious thinker is not only interested in how to change the physical domain, but also why those changes will also change the information domain in a favourable way. The information domain mediates between the physical domain, what humans think and, therefore, what humans do.

If you accept this idea, then things start to get very interesting when we consider how AI interacts in these two domains. The most striking difference, and which explains the tremendous potential of AI, is that AI can directly intervene in the information domain. It does not need to act in the physical world to create an effect in the information domain.

This is because AI exists within the information domain. It is software. An algorithm. AI must be physically instantiated in some way, and it is dependent on the physical world, but it has direct access to the information domain. Humans don't have direct access to that domain (although it is interesting to note that emerging cognitive technologies such as that being developed by companies such as Neuralink may soon change this).

When we are devising strategies to act, we need to consider how we can use AI to influence human behaviour via the information domain, and how we can act in both the physical and information domains to influence AI.

To summarise, there are two approaches to acting:

1. Use humans and AI to act in the physical domain to influence human and AI cognitive processes via the information domain.

2. Use AI to act directly in the information domain to influence human

and AI cognitive processes.

The question then becomes what we decide to do in the information domain to influence human and artificial intellects.

## Faking It

A deepfake is a computer-generated audio or video that portrays a person saying or doing things that never happened. Deepfakes use a machine learning technique called an autoencoder. A good example of deep fake technology in action is a series of clips – available on YouTube – of Sean Connery's face replaced by Burt Reynolds in the James Bond movie Thunderball. The motivation for this deepfake is simple fun: Burt Reynolds turned down the opportunity to play 007. A fan of the movie wondered what the film would have looked like if he hadn't. The results are convincing and illustrate the ease with which AI can be used to fabricate events.

As another example, shortly after the start of the Covid-19 pandemic, Extinction Rebellion (an environmental activist group) generated a deepfake of the Belgian Prime Minister proclaiming a link between deforestation and Covid-19. The video was posted on their Facebook page and was viewed over 100,000 times in less than 24 hrs. According to the journalists who were investigating the video, many comments on the video suggested that people believed the video was authentic.

Deepfakes are a powerful new tool in the propagandists' toolbox. (Interestingly, researchers use the technology that creates deepfakes to also detect them, by looking for subtle, but tell-tale, inconsistencies). An even more powerful tool is OpenAI's GPT-3 technology (which was discussed in

Chapter 4).

What makes GPT-3 particularly powerful is that the user – a human, or another AI – can specify tasks for it to perform. Perhaps you want it to write a completely original text in the style of your favourite author; or to create a website based on other websites that you like. GPT-3 can do all these things and it can do them with only a small amount of input from the user. Nominally less than 10 training examples are required for GPT-3 to learn enough to produce a credible result. Here is an example, from gwern.net, of GPT-3 'writing' a letter to Indiana Jones from his employer[32]:

*Dear Dr. Jones:*

*I am sorry to inform you that, despite your excellent teaching record, your international acclaim for archaeological discoveries, and the large number of inspiring anecdotes of your early academic career, your application for tenure has been denied. In reviewing the numerous reports of your adventures, we were initially struck by your prowess at the site of La Venta, where you single-handedly liberated the Spanish Conquistadors, imprisoned by the wicked god Tezcatlipoca. Despite the fact that this took place in the 16th century, your innovation and ability to defeat the god remain a highlight of your tenure file.*

To be clear, this original work was generated by GPT-3 with only a few prompts by the user. Indeed, the person who tasked GPT-3 with writing this letter described training GPT-3 to do this task as being akin to having a conversation. The humanlike nature of the output from GPT-3 is stark and, for some, unsettling.

It is easy to imagine a future where an algorithm is orchestrating AI to

213

continually perform sentiment analysis on Twitter feeds, whilst also formulating and posting tweets to influence such sentiment. Or AI that is continually monitoring the number of click-throughs from adverts on a website, and re-positioning those adverts and changing the content to find the optimal combination of size, positioning and content.

I say it is easy because *bots* are already a perennial problem on social media; although their lack of sophistication and similarity of content, ironically, reveals that there is a slow human behind the scenes.

Spotting deepfakes from the real thing, human art from AI art or human written texts from AI written texts will become increasingly challenging. Yet, we need to distinguish fact from fake to build an accurate understanding of what is really happening in the world.

## The Rise of Industrial-Scale Intelligence Gathering

What was once the preserve of governments and nations is now emerging as the next critical asset for a business to have. Mitsubishi, one of Japan's largest and most profitable companies, is now investing heavily in building an extensive intelligence network to gain deeper understanding of the markets that they are, or should be, operating in. As Mitsubishi's CEO, Takehiko Kakiuchi, explains '… you have to be a very international company to catch all the global developments that are changing by the second…'[33]

He is not wrong. Even superpowers must enlist help in building an intelligence network, sometimes with embarrassing and damaging consequences. In late September 2020, Anne-Marie Brady at the The

214

Washington Post, broke the news that a small Chinese company, called Zhenhua Data Information Technology, had been collecting information on prominent individuals around the world.

Now, that fact on its own isn't too surprising, it was the scale of their endeavour that was extraordinary – 2.4 million people covering every country or territory in the world. This small company – that includes Chinese defence and intelligence agencies on its client list – had built a significant intelligence asset for the Chinese government, to inform the *who, what, where,* and *when* from which they could plan to act in the world.

## Be Careful What You Wish For

Sometimes, when deploying tactics to manipulate markets or public opinion, things can backfire or – at least – have negative unintended consequences.

A recent example is when the chip manufacturer, Nvidia, recently launched their Ampere range of graphics cards. As with any new tech product from a major manufacturer, there was a considerable amount of hype; however, for this launch, the hype seemed particularly high. The reason was simple: Nvidia were proclaiming to be delivering a product that had better performance than its last flagship product for nearly half the price.

This highly compelling combination of price-to-performance was enough to bring Nvidia's own website to its knees at 2pm on Thursday 17th September 2020 when the product was launched. Many small resellers' websites also could not cope with the volume of traffic to their site. Surveys on enthusiast forums once the dust had settled showed that only 12% of people had successfully secured the product. What is more, once resellers had managed to regain control of their websites, they realised that they had received orders that far outstripped their ability to deliver (including Amazon). Cue mass cancellations of orders.

This led many people – as voiced everywhere from Twitter, Facebook, Reddit to those dedicated enthusiast forums – to question what on earth had gone so wrong. Either Nvidia were as surprised as anyone about the popularity of their product or there was a significant problem in the manufacturing of the product. Or so-called 'scalpers' had taken everything that was available (these are people who use automated algorithms to buy all available stock within milliseconds of a product going live and then sell the product for a significant profit on eBay). Or something else was afoot.

The nom de plume 'Moore's Law is Dead' (MLID) is an insider in the semiconductor chip industry. Quite presciently, a few days before the Nvidia launch (which, incidentally, was shrouded in mystery with very few leaks of information), MLID wrote a blog post called *Nvidia's Ultimate Play* in which he described how Nvidia would artificially constrain supply of their new product, the Geforce RTX 3800, which was hitting that magical price/performance ratio to meet market demand.

Why would they do this? MLID cited an industry veteran who informed him that Nvidia were making a move to 'have their cake and eat it too'. Nvidia's previous product range – called Turing – was much maligned by most of their customers as the price/performance ratio was not hitting the sweet spot. Nvidia had a brand image problem: if you want high performance then you must pay for it.

Now, it is true that Nvidia produced the highest performing graphics cards in the world, but they were expensive. Ordinarily, Nvidia would probably have stuck to the mantra of you get what you pay for; however, in Autumn 2020, their biggest rival, AMD, were set to launch their new product range – called Big Navi – with performance rumoured to exceed Nvidia's previous flagship Turing product.

This got Nvidia worried and so a plan was hatched to make customers believe Nvidia had solved the price/performance problem with their Ampere range. Furthermore, they were going to launch six weeks ahead of AMD's Big Navi product range. MLID claimed that Nvidia knew this was not a sustainable price but didn't want to put the price up as that would just re-confirm everyone's belief that Nvidia was the more expensive rival of AMD.

So how to get the price to where it met Nvidia's profit targets whilst absolving Nvidia of any blame? Create artificial supply and demand. Most consumers know that if demand for a product is high, but supply is limited, then the price goes up. What better way to do this than to artificially constrain production of a massively hyped product? The launch of Ampere played out as predicted by MLID. As of the end of January 2021 it is still not possible to buy these products and yet more expensive third-party versions are in abundant supply.

Whether this really was Nvidia's strategy – or whether MLID has a fantastic imagination – the fallout has damaged the loyalty of Nvidia's fan base as they feel manipulated and even betrayed by the company. Meanwhile their biggest rival, AMD, took steps to launch their own suite of new products, hitting that magical price/performance ratio.

Opinions on Nvidia's perceived treachery to its customers – whether justified or not – continues on all major social media platforms and specialist forums. The internet has a long memory, and it remains to be seen whether Nvidia's gains from short-term manipulation of the market outweighed the loss of customers. It also remains to be seen whether MLID was right.

One thing is certain though: Nvidia did not attempt to engage with customers to explain why the launch of the Ampere range had gone so spectacularly bad for their loyal customer base. That is a curious decision.

If Nvidia had more of the capabilities described in this book – forecasting the $2^{nd}$ order, $3^{rd}$ order, $n^{th}$ order effects of such a strategy before committing to it – would they have still proceeded as they did?

## Making Good Decisions when Information Is Available

Decision science is about making optimal choices from the information that is currently available. The focus is on using existing knowledge to inform a decision; not to pursue new knowledge.

In seeking to achieve an optimal decision, the veracity and provenance of information that is being used to inform that decision is of particular importance. Furthermore, a degree of analytical rigour is expected with alternative options being considered and an optimal option selected based on the evidence available, and the anticipated benefit compared to the associated risks and costs. Clearly, the aim is to maximise the benefit of that decision whilst minimising the risks and the costs.

The healthcare sector is a good example of decision science in practice. In making a diagnosis and deciding on a course of treatment, Medical Doctors consult guidelines set by their industry. Some doctors may also undertake their own independent research (ideally peer-reviewed and published) and include the results in their decision-making.

Knowledge in the healthcare sector is largely based on a statistical approach. You only have to read any kind of medical journal to see the prevalence of phrases such as '32% in the control group therefore with a $p$ value of 0.03' to see the foundation of statistics in decision-making in this sector. Interestingly, AI – in the form of expert systems – has been used in the healthcare sector for decades to aid doctors in making decisions.

The key point is that decision science is aimed at using data to inform specific, well-defined decisions: What should we invest in over the next three years? Which demographic of the voting population should we target? When would be the best time for us to launch this new product?

Decision science is about what to do, when to do it, and where to do it. Sometimes decisions can be made confidently based on the data available, with confident predictions of an outcome. Most of the time there is less confidence in an outcome and so, in the process of deciding, more questions need to be answered first. For example, in deciding which demographic of the voting population to target with highly tailored messages, there may be insufficient knowledge. The decision-making process may therefore require small, quick experiments to generate new knowledge required to arrive at a good decision.

Dr Chris Dowsett, Head of Decision Science at Instagram, has talked about how Instagram have both data scientists and decision scientists. The data scientists focus on the data and complex analysis, while the decision scientists focus on using subject-matter expertise in a particular product or service to help management make good decisions.

The economists Ajay Agrawal, Joshua Gans and Avi Goldfarb, in their book *Prediction Machines*, offer the *AI Canvas* as a model for understanding how AI can help with a business decision. The AI canvas is a brainstorming tool to understand what is required to make a decision and to identify the data required to support that decision. Their tool combines specifying what needs to be predicted and the cost of getting that prediction wrong; and subsequently identifying what action to take that could lead to an intended outcome. The sequence of predict → judge cost → act → outcome are the essential components of a decision. Supporting that decision-making sequence is data, referred to as input, training and feedback data – as generally expected for a machine learning algorithm.

## Types of Decisions

Carl Spetzler describes the information space in which decisions take place as the amount of data available vs. the degree of evidence driving a decision. Within this information space there are three types of decisions: Automatic, Operational and Strategic.

Where there is a very large amount of data in the information space, this lends itself to potential automation. The use of machine learning for applications such as driverless cars, or tweaking user experience by automatically changing the position of an advert on a Google search are examples of automatic decision-making.

Where there is access to some data, but not sufficient to fully automate decision-making, then data can provide insights and recommendations to inform a decision.

Where access to data is limited, mainly due to the nature of the task in hand – for example, strategic planning or long-term forecasting – whatever data is relevant and available may provide insight.

Within the language of Pearl's Ladder of Causation, one can see that Imagination is likely to be a causal discovery activity at the Strategic level, and significantly less so at the Automatic level. Conversely, Association is more likely to be useful at the Automatic level. It may also be that Intervention modes of reasoning are most useful at the Operational level, where corrective action is often required.

The nature of decisions made at each of these levels should be different. For example, we may want to have highly structured decision-making processes at the Automated level, that then become increasingly unstructured at the Strategic level. There is a clear overlap here with the 'wisdom hierarchy' that I described in Chapter 3.

## Acquiring Data

If we accept that the information domain is the primary environment within which to seek to create an effect that can change human or AI behaviour, then we are reliant on data that informs our understanding of that domain. There are four sources of data:

**Open source.** This is data that is in the public domain and accessible to everyone. Some of this data may be curated and provided at an additional cost but, overall, if you know what you are looking for then you have a good chance of finding it. Examples of open source information are the internet, the media, professional and academic publications, reports, and government data. However, open source data can also reside in the deep web which, because standard search engines do not index this part of the web, are not so easily accessed. Yet highly valuable data could reside there if you know how to navigate it.

The main attractions of open source data are the cost (most of it is freely available), the ease with which it can be obtained, and access to insights that others have gained into that same data (for example, the multiple, simultaneous analyses worldwide based on Covid-19 data released by the World Health Organisation).

**Third-party.** This is data that another organisation has gathered and made available for others to purchase. Arrangements to access the data vary from vendor to vendor. Facebook, for example, allow customers to buy access to their Facebook Analyse suite where Facebook's tools are used to search their social network and to act within it, such as placing adverts. Other third-party vendors could be specialist data analysis companies, such as Recorded Futures, who are expert at navigating and acquiring data from the deep web.

**Proprietary.** This is data that an organisation generates from its own operations. This could be data about customers, suppliers, the workforce, or data about production facilities, distribution networks, and so on. It is easy to assume that proprietary data is of the highest value and utility, however, this isn't necessarily the case. It costs money to maintain a product, service or platform that is generating data. It also costs money to store, process and analyse that data.

The tools and computing resources required also cost money, and so does having a skilled workforce able to proficiently maintain an end-to-end data platform (from ingesting data through to using insights from that data to inform decisions).

**Synthetic.** If you have identified a need for data but have no means to collect it in sufficient quantities or of an acceptable quality then, for some uses, you could look to synthesise the data. As I mentioned in Chapter 4, before Tesla Inc. became a major car manufacturer, they used computer simulations and synthesised data to train their AutoPilot AI technology. It helped them to get going with their self-driving ambitions. Synthesised data allows you to explore counterfactuals; it allows you to extrapolate or interpolate from a spare real-world dataset, and so on. But synthesised data does need to be used with caution. The data scientist generating the dataset may unintentionally introduce bias by defining certain types of data that will be generated. There are also more obvious risks to over-relying on synthetic data: it is not representative of real-world data which tends to be significantly more complex, varied and surprising.

For example, Tesla Inc. noticed that the real world is extremely random at times and it is almost impossible to predict events such that they can be modelled (e.g., a tyre bouncing across the road in front of a self-driving car, or a bicycle falling off the bike rack of the car in front). Subsequently, the performance of machine learning models that have lived on an exclusive diet of synthetic data may fall far short when deployed in the real world.

According to Statista's 2019 report on the Market Technology industry, the most trusted source of data that marketers use to inform their actions is their partners. The second most trusted is in-house data created by their own research or data science teams. Significantly fewer marketeers trust data from tech companies, publishers or media firms.

There is a clear cost/benefit decision regarding which of these data sources to invest in and it can be tricky to figure out where to start. With clients, I start with the simple question: what decisions do you need to make? As I begin to explore that question – usually with a senior leader and their top team – what comes out are a set of top-level use-cases (a use-case is simply a description of an activity that someone performs to achieve a task).

Once a use-case has been captured we can then work backwards from that to identify the questions that need to be answered to support that decision. Those questions define the insights that are required from data to support a good quality decision. With a decision-centric view on data, the return on investment in data is clearer and more traceable.

For an organisation pursuing a cognitive advantage trajectory, I would expect to see the following questions:

Is our operating environment changing in a way that we need to pay more attention to it?

What are our competitors doing?

What products or services are our customers purchasing?

Some of the decisions:

When should we launch this new product?

Should we buy this company? If we do what are the likely consequences? Are those possible future scenarios acceptable?

Should we proceed with this policy? If we do what are the likely consequences? Are those possible future scenarios acceptable?

However, there are some unexpected decisions that have a significant impact. In such circumstances we may find ourselves with little supporting data or evidence. An essential quality of the underlying data architecture, therefore, is the ability to pivot the organisation's data aperture to incorporate critical data needed to inform decisions. If no data is available then it may be a case of proceeding carefully with small, thoughtful and insightful experiments to generate the datapoints that may yield the required insight to reach a decision.

This is why some of the most data and tech savvy firms in the world – Instagram for example – employ decision scientists. They can interpret urgent and important decisions into a clearly defined data ask.

## Ethical Use of Data and AI

The technology and infrastructure for acquiring significant amounts of data, from which to extract precise insights about people's behaviours has been commoditised and made available and accessible to anyone. However, there are serious ethical implications for the use of data related to privacy and security.

Mandy Chessell, a Distinguished Engineer at IBM, has developed a big data and analytics ethics framework. At the heart of this framework is a question: what is the ethical position of the organisation with respect to the use of data? There are three sub-questions: what is technically possible, what is legal, and what are we trying to achieve? An ethical position is the point at which the answer to those three questions converges.

Chessell recommends that an ethical decision is one where the following topics have been demonstrably considered and recorded (which she refers to as the ethical awareness framework):

**Context.** Why was the data originally collected? How is it now being used? What is the difference?

**Consent and Choice.** Is the affected party (a person, an organisation) aware that this data is being collected and have they consented to this? Do they know they have made that choice?

**Reasonable.** Is the data that is being collected and used proportionate to the need?

**Substantiated.** Is the data appropriate, complete and timely for its intended use? (If not, then why collect and store it?)

**Owned.** Who owns the insights gained from this data?

**Fair.** Are affected parties appropriately compensated? (For example, Facebook may argue that their users get free access to their platform)

**Considered.** Has sufficient thought been given to the consequences of the collection and analysis of this data?

**Access.** What access to data and analysis of that data does the affected party have?

**Accountable.** How will mistakes be rectified and reported?

In October 2019, the UK's Royal Society of Arts and Google's AI company, DeepMind, engaged with the general public to discuss AI. Through this engagement – using an approach that the RSA called a citizens' jury – a toolkit was developed for how to develop ethical AI. The toolkit is publicly available and described in their report, *Democratising decisions about technology: a toolkit.*

In March 2021 the UK's Government Communications Headquarters (GCHQ) announced their AI ethics framework and the legal provisions within which their organisation operates with data and AI. Fairness, Transparency & Accountability are the main components of their AI ethics decision-making framework. These are similar to the basis of IBM's AI ethics framework: the properties of explainability, fairness, robustness, transparency and privacy.

The General Data Protection Regulation (GDPR) was brought into effect in 2018 by the European Union with the aim of giving individuals control over how their personal data is used by companies and governments.

The legislation also requires organisations to report any breaches to the individual concerned and to a regulatory authority (in the UK this is the Information Commissioner's Office). The directive requires organisations that retain data on people to demonstrate that their business processes are compliant with such practices. In a review in 2020, the EU stated that GDPR had been a success in its first 2 years of operation.

Whilst GDPR has introduced important regulatory controls across industry and government, it only shows that an organisation is compliant with the control of personal data. It doesn't convey any notion of how ethically an organisation is using that data. Perhaps it is time for a kitemark, or other symbol of quality, that clearly indicates that an organisation is demonstrably practising an ethical code of conduct in their use of data. In a sense, along with GDPR compliance, such an ethical kitemark could become an important and necessary attribute, considered mandatory by customers, suppliers and the workforce.

Finally, we must consider the ethics of human action.

In the latter half of the 20<sup>th</sup> century and even now in the early 21<sup>st</sup> century, the ability to win at all costs has been the main compass by which we laud and reward our leaders. Maximising shareholder value or winning votes has been the largely unquestioned aim and a board that is responsible to its shareholders or to party members needs the best person for that job. Action happens, but is it wise action? Ethical work practices and caring about people from a more human perspective, became secondary, or fell away altogether. Using an algorithm to judge a human workforce – such as

Amazon's infamous 'the rate' algorithm, which has led to mental health issues in the workforce – is a stark reminder that AI can introduce new, unintended consequences.

As AI is increasingly used to augment and enhance the cognitive capabilities of decision-makers, it becomes supremely important that our leaders of tomorrow have a strong foundation of ethics and morality.

The Greeks and the Romans placed emphasis on the qualities of a good leader. In *Meditations*, the Roman Emperor Marcus Aurelius said, 'Don't think about being a good person, just be that good person'[34]. He cited attributes such as wisdom, morality, moderation and courage. We need to set greater expectations for our leaders along these lines.

We may think of a sagacious leader as someone who embodies such values whilst also having the innate ability to process complex information – ambiguous, volatile, incomplete – to inform action that has profound impact. Oftentimes such decisions may be tactical, short-term and immediate. But the sagacious leader is also comfortable with the abstract, and with developing strategy shaped by ethos.

With the right mix of minds, better decisions can be made; a more well-rounded leadership team gives a deeper, more insightful, more morally balanced view of the major strategic decisions that their organisation needs to make.

Different perspectives are essential to arriving at the most sagacious actions.

# Chapter 8
# The Cognitive Enterprise

*'It is only with prudence, sagacity, and much dexterity that great aims are accomplished...* '[35]

Napoleon Bonaparte

A cognitive enterprise is an organisation that prioritises deeply insightful and far-sighted action to shape an operating environment as the means for success. The cognitive enterprise specialises in the fusion of AI with human intelligence, within a culture that venerates knowledge, creativity and wise action. The result is an enterprise that can out-think, out-manoeuvre and out-innovate the competition by gaining and maintaining a cognitive advantage.

A cognitive enterprise provides the ability to sense and act at such a speed that no one else can keep up; and for those actions to have an impact that is disproportionate to the level of effort and resource put into them. Competitors find it too hard and too expensive to keep up, and consequently get left further and further behind.

The cognitive enterprise is an organisation that is truly augmented by AI. It is in the DNA of the organisation itself, built from the ground up. So, what should a cognitive enterprise be good at? Recurring throughout the previous chapters were the following points:

- Sense, think and move faster than your adversaries and maximise the use of AI to do this

- Optimise human and AI working together in a symbiotic way and design cognitive tools into workflows

- Actively shape the operating environment and connect deeply into both the physical and information domains (you cannot sense and act without connecting in some way)

- Be sagacious in how you act in your dependent ecosystems and cultivate long-term sustainability

- Venerate learning and knowledge, invest in it, and efficiently apply it to solve problems and make decisions

- Decentralise and autonomise as far and as widely as possible but without losing accountability

- Be sufficiently self-aware of the fit of your organisation to your operating environment

- Instil values of curiosity and audacity alongside ancient values of moderation, morality, courage and wisdom

There are an almost unlimited number of ways in which a cognitive enterprise could be designed to embody these, or other, principles. Modern management thinking and practices – such as agile methodologies, knowledge and data management, team-of-teams, and so on – remain relevant and useful. But the cognitive enterprise should call for new thinking too.

We may start by considering the following design goals for the cognitive enterprise:

Goal 1        Significantly increase the capability and capacity of human intellect to reason and act optimally

Goal 2        Allow AI to ascend and excel at all levels of the Ladder of Causation

And in pursuit of those goals, the following sub-goals have been identified; they relate to each level of the Ladder of Causation:

Goal 3        Maximise the use of AI to automate 'Association' reasoning

Goal 4        Use AI to assist and catalyse the creative and problem-solving activities of humans… and other AI

Goal 5        Ensure that humans and machines can search, read and share the same information, with access to the same supporting tools

I have identified concepts that are sufficiently novel, and potentially useful, as to warrant explanation here. These are the principles around which to design a cognitive enterprise: (1) cognitive agents that are, (2) supported by a synthetic core that, (3) sustains the enterprise as a living system.

## Principle 1. The Cognitive Agent

The cognitive enterprise is a form of organisation that is centred on informed dialogue and decision-making by the right people, equipped with unique data insights and augmented by artificial intelligence. A key motivation is to reserve human time and effort to those activities that we are best suited to; ingenuity, wisdom and compassion. Such a human-centric ethos is pre-eminent in designing the cognitive enterprise. To make the best use of human time, artificial and human intellects must be combined to form a collective intelligence. This intelligence will drive the most efficacious collective action to maintain the organisation within a window of viability.

In engineering terms, when we are designing a system, we need to understand the constituent parts of that system, and we need to understand what we are measuring in order to understand the performance of the system and whether it is adhering to specifications. As we design a cognitive enterprise, we need to define the fundamental unit of analysis – the atomic, indivisible unit. In an enterprise where the aim is to constantly understand how the environment is changing and what that might mean, there are cognitive processes – either human or machine – that enable us to do that. The concept of a cognitive agent could be the fundamental unit of the cognitive enterprise.

As we begin to design a cognitive enterprise to achieve these goals, it may be useful to have a focal point. Given that the aim of the cognitive enterprise is to orchestrate a collective intelligence, we should perhaps start by looking at the entities that make up a collective intelligence – the cognitive agent.

A 'unit of analysis' is the thing, or object, that frames the focus of what is being studied. In this case, the cognitive agent is the object of study. By understanding what a cognitive agent is and how it needs to operate, we can begin to design our cognitive enterprise to fully enable that entity to operate in an optimal way. So, let's start at the beginning: what is a cognitive agent?

We could define a cognitive agent as an autonomous, intelligent entity that is pursuing a goal and executing a series of tasks that enable it to do so:

**Functional**      A cognitive agent behaves as an intelligent entity whereby it is making sense of its environment, reasoning about what that means for the pursuit of its goal, and determining and acting accordingly

**Descriptive**     A cognitive agent has attributes and functions, some of which are visible to other cognitive agents, and some which are not

**Conceptual**      A cognitive agent is an autopoietic system (described in Chapter 3) that is continually maintaining its own integrity to ensure its ability to endure in pursuit of its goal

A cognitive agent must have an ability to:

- Capture and Observe (Pattern recognition)

- Hypothesise and Experiment (Create)

- Imagine and Reflect (Counterfactual reasoning)

- Learn and Remember (Associate)

- Devise and Act (Intervene)

- Communicate with other cognitive agents (Collaborate and Exchange)

- Maintain the optimal working of the above functions (Autopoiesis)

Any entity – machine or human – that fulfils these criteria is deemed to be a cognitive agent. The engineering aims of building the cognitive enterprise are to enable many cognitive agents to fulfil these functions.

## The Confluence of Skills, Knowledge, Data and Tools

In early 2019 I was helping a client develop their digital transformation strategy and we settled – as most others do – on the importance of making the best use of data or, to be a bit more buzz-wordy about it, being data-driven. We then unpacked that phrase further: what does it mean to be data driven? (Answer: You excel at using data to be more competitive.) Does that artificially constrain our thinking by assuming that if an activity can't be captured as data then it is of no value? (Answer: Yes that is a consequence, but you won't know the impact of that until you start the journey.)

Now, whilst the answers to those questions were still playing out, the more practical question we arrived at was: how do we make best use of our people working with data? I drew the following diagram:

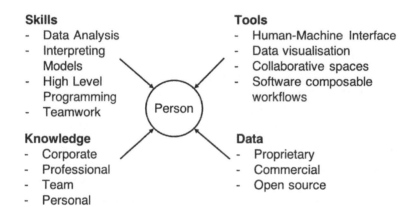

**Skills**
- Data Analysis
- Interpreting Models
- High Level Programming
- Teamwork

**Knowledge**
- Corporate
- Professional
- Team
- Personal

**Tools**
- Human-Machine Interface
- Data visualisation
- Collaborative spaces
- Software composable workflows

**Data**
- Proprietary
- Commercial
- Open source

Person

*Figure 15. The human decision-maker as the focal point in the design and engineering of an enterprise architecture*

'Our job', I said, 'is to design the organisation in a way that we maximise the effectiveness of how these four things come together to help someone do their job better'.

The unspoken implication here is that a person's job has value. Using this simple arrangement allowed the client to focus on providing the best possible experience to its people. In a sense, whilst the over-arching aim for their digital transformation was to become more data-driven, the strategy to achieve that was people-centric. With the notion of a cognitive agent the

237

logic is the same and extends to focus on artificial agents as much as human ones. Hence, whereas a good digital transformation strategy should be people-centric, a good cognitive advantage strategy should be intellect-centric. With this in mind, we can now modify and extend the people-centric concept to:

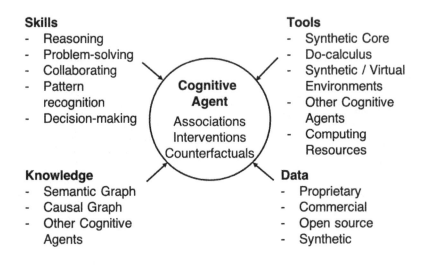

**Skills**
- Reasoning
- Problem-solving
- Collaborating
- Pattern recognition
- Decision-making

**Knowledge**
- Semantic Graph
- Causal Graph
- Other Cognitive Agents

**Cognitive Agent**
Associations
Interventions
Counterfactuals

**Tools**
- Synthetic Core
- Do-calculus
- Synthetic / Virtual Environments
- Other Cognitive Agents
- Computing Resources

**Data**
- Proprietary
- Commercial
- Open source
- Synthetic

*Figure 16. The cognitive agent as the focal point in the design and engineering of an enterprise architecture*

As can be seen in Figure 16, the four categories remain the same. What has changed is the detail of what skills, what knowledge, what tools and what data are now important to optimise the performance of a cognitive agent.

I propose that a cognitive agent is a minimal autopoietic system within the organisation: it has a goal, it has the means to make sense of its environment, and it also has the means to act in its environment with the goal of maintaining its identity and persisting for as long as its goal is relevant. The concept of a cognitive agent gives us a unit of analysis – an identifiable asset that we can invest in, and that generates value for the organisation. The specific cognitive function can be performed by a human, or an AI, or a fusion of the two. The key criterion is that it is a self-sustaining structure that delivers an indivisible cognitive function within the organisation.

A cognitive agent must incorporate an artificial intellect as much as a human intellect. When we talk in terms of maximising the cognitive potential of an organisation, we must talk about AI in the same tone and with the same intent as we would human intellect.

It is important to pay attention to the outputs of our cognitive agents – especially as environments change at an ever-increasing rate. How many times have we heard about an employee, probably an engineer, in a huge organisation inventing something which senior management dismiss because they believe it isn't relevant, and it then turns out to be the piece of key technology that completely disrupts the industry five years down the line?

Cognitive agents need to have the freedom to explore hypotheses, to give the best chance of anticipating how the environment is likely to change, and therefore how to best prepare for that; and then to take action that prepares for that change. Frequently there is a dual purpose for a technology.

It might have been invented and used for one purpose but is then found to be highly useful for another purpose. To harness this possibility, a cognitive agent is given the means, and is almost expected, to be constantly exploring the 'adjacent possible'[36], to use Stuart Kauffman's term.

The cognitive agent is a manifestation of the elements of cognition we have discussed so far; it brings them together into a construct that we can then start designing organisations around. To put this into everyday language, we need to get the right data to the right people – to optimise the relationship between data, people and tools (including AI).

We need to maximise the creative skills of people, using powerful tools like AI, to work with data to make sense of the environment in order to operate in such a way that the organisation succeeds. Understanding the mechanisms by which this happens in an AI-rich world requires delving into some abstract concepts; on a higher level, however, we can use more readily accessible concepts to describe the design and function of the cognitive enterprise.

## A Decision-Centric Architecture

A cognitive enterprise should prioritise sagacious decision-making. That is, decisions that are made with deep insight into context and consequences. Figure 17 is an illustration of what a high-level decision-centric architecture may look like. There are five major components to this model: the decision-making process; a set of influencing factors; a human-to-machine or machine-to-machine interface; a knowledge discovery and exploitation platform; and a knowledge platform.

## Decision-Making Process

The decision-making process is structured around a Perception-Action Loop (as discussed in Chapter 3) with activities including:

**Sense-making.** A process of trying to make sense of the world so that we can act in it. We need to have a sufficient understanding of the current situation to begin to formulate an action. So, we seek to identify, recognise and evaluate events that are happening, or that may happen, or that have happened. We also seek to project what might happen next. We infer from the current situation in order to predict or anticipate what may happen next. We are seeking to identify the nature of the decision that may be required. We may need to search for and use additional information to help us reach such an understanding.

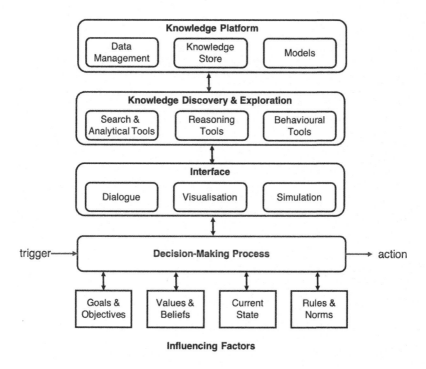

*Figure 17. The basic architectural components of decision-making*

**Meaning-making.** How we understand, or make sense of, the present situation and what that may mean for the future. Meaning-making is intimately tied to our sense of self, our identity. How does the current situation relate to our goals, ambitions, purpose? Meaning-making evaluates what we are making sense of. How does this compare to my own beliefs? Is it surprising or expected? How might this affect me? Once we attach a meaning to the current situation, we begin to formulate a decision: what are we going to do about it?

**Evaluating Options.** Once we have made sense of a situation, we begin to identify options. Do I do $a$ or $b$ or $c$? In evaluating options, we need more information. We form hypotheses: if I do $a$ then the outcome should be $x$. How confident do I feel about that? What may prevent that from happening? The more complex the situation, the harder it is to have any certainty that $a$ will lead to $x$, or that $b$ will lead to $y$, and so on. Tools to help decision-making include predictive models, forecasting models, simulations, and insights from data. Oftentimes a perfectly acceptable conclusion from a decision-making process is to not do anything.

**Synthesising Action.** Once we have decided on a course of action, we need to construct how we execute that action. In basic terms, what do we need to do? Who else may we need to task? Who do we need to tell? What do we need to move? We plan. Tools to help synthesise an action are planning tools, stakeholder analysis, simulations. Where AI is performing automated decisions, it would refer to a policy of pre-approved limits or bounds to act with compliance.

As we begin to implement our plans, we begin to have an effect. The effect of our actions will trigger another decision-making loop where we, once again, make sense of the situation, evaluate options, and act.

## Influencing Factors

**Goals and Objectives.** The aims of the individual, or the AI agent, that is seeking to make a decision. The goals and objectives frame the decision and contribute towards higher goals of the organisation that tend to be longer term. We attach meaning to a situation by evaluating how it compares to our goals and objectives.

**Values and Beliefs.** The personality of the individual that shapes their behaviour. Their preferences. Their sense of purpose. Their values and beliefs strongly influence the meaning they attach to a situation and therefore what sense they make of it.

**Current State.** The present state of the individual: are they stressed or relaxed? The present situation: is the task in hand important and urgent, complex or simple? How knowable is the current situation? How determinable is the outcome of an action? Is information available and of sufficient quality? Is the situation ambiguous and uncertain? In other words, what level of complexity is the individual operating in at that time? AI will not be affected by an emotional state. However, the performance of the AI in making a good decision will be affected by the same environmental issues as the human.

**Rules and Norms.** The policies of the organisation; operating in a way that is compliant with those policies. These introduce constraints and guidance for the individual making the decision. AI will also be bound by policy constraints. Our values and beliefs may either reinforce these rules and norms, or we may rail against them. If we are for the rules, then this can simplify action. If we are against the rules, then we tend to have to work harder to justify an action. Hence, developing policies that best align to what is needed can make decision-making more efficient.

## Interface

The ideal is to design a suite of tools and products that provides an immersive, seamless, natural experience, allowing the cognitive agent to efficiently retrieve, read and reason with complex and multi-dimensional data and multimedia. Fields of research such as neuro-ergonomics should find increasing utility here. Furthermore, the interface should be a continually improved experience that uses AI to learn about the thinking style and preferences of the cognitive agent and adapt the user experience accordingly.

**Dialogue.** Verbal and written communication with other people or with AI (using natural language processing). Communication with AI should be in the form of questions and instructions, as exemplified by smart assistants like Alexa, Cortana, Siri, and so on. Communication with people should be optimised through understanding and embracing the principles of dialectics and Stacey's complex responsive processes.

**Visualisation.** A broad range of tools to visualise data, knowledge or structure of a system. The focus is on presenting complex information in a succinct way. Technologies such as Augmented Reality and Virtual Reality are relevant here.

**Simulation.** A synthetic environment that provides a consistent interface to a wide range of simulations of models. For example, mathematical models, Digital Twins, 3D models, forecasting models, and so on. The synthetic

244

environment allows users to experiment, play, problem solve, learn, and explore through computer simulations.

## Knowledge Discovery and Exploration

A human or a machine is querying the knowledge store, exploring concepts and generating new knowledge from comprehending existing knowledge. AI is autonomously exploring possible causal connections, generating hypotheses and synthesising possible experiments to test that hypothesis.

**Knowledge Search and Analysis.** Search and retrieval of items from the knowledge store. Data science tools and methods to query data, information and knowledge. Prediction and forecasting tools.

**Reasoning.** Tools for supporting deduction and inference. Concepts such as Pearl's Ladder of Causation (Associating, Intervening, Imagining) should be implemented as a methodology for accelerated and assisted reasoning. Machine Learning and AI should make a significant contribution here.

**Behavioural Analysis.** Tools for understanding motivation and behaviours of people. This can be to aid comprehension – for example, why someone has behaved in a certain way – or to aid the formulation of strategies and tactics to influence behaviours.

## Knowledge Platform

**Data Management.** A system for managing the complete lifecycle of an item of data from when the data is captured, or acquired, through to deletion of the data. Such governance of the data, including access control, auditing, logging and traceability. Other functions include tagging, or labelling of data, recording and updating data catalogues, assessment of data quality, the provenance and veracity of data. The data management platform provides a compliant and quality-assured foundation for the cognitive enterprise.

**Knowledge Store.** A semantic graph that contains all the knowledge about the organisation including its operations, products and services, customers, competitors, partners and the broader operating environment.

**Models.** The library of models ranging from structural causal models through to learning models used by machine learning and AI. The management of the lifecycle of each model in the library.

## Principle 2. The Synthetic Core

The critical centre of the cognitive enterprise should consist of an accessible and simulated digital version of itself and its operating environment (which I refer to as the synthetic core) – an encoded representation of everything that the organisation has learned and continues to learn about itself and its environment. This body of knowledge and meaning is queried, explored and updated by the collective intelligence of the organisation.

In the cognitive enterprise, we maximise learning and minimise cost and risk by allowing AI to run their own simulations – experiments – as far as possible in a synthetic environment designed and tested to be as close as possible a match for the real environment. In this way the AI is acting like a human – except much, much faster. It is looking at different creative approaches to have maximum impact in its environment. We need to give it the ability to experiment and explore, safely and quickly, before it commits to a real-world action.

The synthetic core is a system of automated knowledge management, from discovering new knowledge to 'gardening' existing knowledge. The concept is based on a simple premise: use AI to optimise our knowledge about everything that is relevant, or that may be relevant, to us. New techniques such as meta machine learning, or open-ended machine learning, may be of use here.

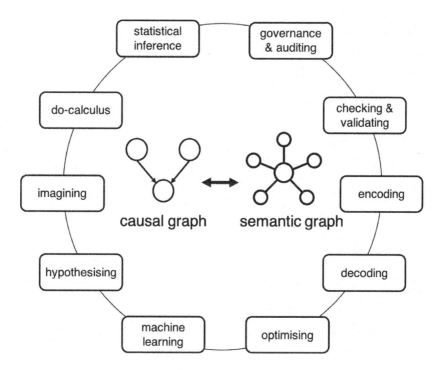

*Figure 18. The Synthetic Core embodies everything that the collective intelligence of the organisation knows about the world that it operates in.*

The aim of the synthetic core is to optimise the organisation's knowledge through:

- Automated maintenance of the organisation's semantic graph and causal graph

- Automated discovery of new knowledge through exhaustive exploration of, and experimentation with, existing knowledge

The synthetic core (as illustrated in Figure 18) consists of two critical assets: a semantic graph and a causal graph. The combination of these two graphs provides a rich model of elements in the world (semantic graph) of interest to the organisation, and how this world behaves (causal graph). I believe the semantic graph has precedence over the causal graph as it should be the encoded representation of all that we know about the world that our organisation operates in.

The causal graph seeks to explain how entities within that world behave with respect to each other and, from this, we gain new insights. Whilst I have shown these assets as single entities, they could both be instantiated in whatever way is deemed most appropriate to a particular organisation or group of cooperating organisations e.g., as part of a federated architecture.

Both knowledge assets are maintained and updated by automated algorithms. The complexity of these graphs – their size, their interconnectedness, the speed with which they change – means that humans are probably not a good solution here. Hence, I advocate for AI to be the custodians of these critical corporate assets.

As can be seen from Figure 18, I have suggested ten functions – all performed or used by AI or automated algorithms. These illustrate the kind of activities that may be required to perform automated knowledge discovery and knowledge maintenance. How this is instantiated in the real world should differ for each organisation and should be designed to best suit the context of that organisation. The causal discovery functions – imagining, hypothesising, statistical inference, do-calculus – were described in Chapter 4.

The custodial functions – governance and auditing, checking and validating, encoding and decoding – should be the same as any robust conventional knowledge management platform. The optimisation function should identify opportunities to discover new knowledge and improve the quality of existing knowledge. It should task other functions within the synthetic core, and the data access functions of the enterprise (that is, to signify what data is required that is not currently being supplied to the synthetic core). The machine learning function should be a suite of learning and optimisation algorithms made available to all other functions within the synthetic core.

## Principle 3. The Cognitive Enterprise as a Living System

In pursuing the principles of the cognitive enterprise, it is important to realise that any organisation is a living system. In Chapter 3 I talked about autopoiesis as being the characteristic that distinguishes a living system from a non-living system i.e., one that persists through adaptation and self-maintenance. a system that persists from one that doesn't. A living system must have a degree of autonomy, and because it has a degree of autonomy it has a degree of unpredictability; and unpredictability leads to novelty and the discovery of new things.

One of the design principles of the cognitive enterprise is to recognise that our unit of analysis is the cognitive agent; and the cognitive agent is defined as an autopoietic system. An autopoietic system is an autonomous system that is pursuing a particular goal; it can adapt, and it seeks to maintain itself and maintain its relevance within a window of viability. That brings together the points we have talked about in previous chapters.

For people who design organisations, the starting point is to think about the cognitive functions and the cognitive agents, and how to best optimise the success of the cognitive agents by making sure they have access to the right cognitive functions as and when they need them.

When people talk about an organisation, they tend to think about wiring diagrams, with the Chief Exec at the top, then the Vice President, then the divisions – a very command and control structure. That simply doesn't make sense for a cognitive enterprise. The best way to understand the structure of a cognitive enterprise is as a complex network – because there is a high degree of uncertainty about what that network might do, collectively, at any point in time.

The nodes in this network are the cognitive agents, those autonomous entities pursuing their own goals, and the edges between the nodes are the information transfer.

The topology of the network will have many feedback loops, which is what makes it so uncertain. A fundamental concept, therefore, is to design the organisation to be a complex network, not as functional silos. Every cognitive agent will be trying to make sense of its environment, and the enterprise itself will form part of the environment of that cognitive agent.

By explicitly acknowledging these feedback loops, their uncertainty and the fact that they will constitute a complex network, we recognise their importance and we can begin to design for them, and advance strategies for how we are going to build our cognitive enterprise.

The organisation will have thousands, if not millions, of perception-action loops going on asynchronously and distributed with very little central control. In fact, there probably won't be much control at all. They will be driven much more by goals – defined by human-valued principles, desires, needs and preferences.

There is a degree of unpredictability in how such systems will act; so, one of the challenges of the cognitive enterprise is how to marshal, guide and enable the community of autopoietic systems in such a way that they have the freedom to excel within their function, and to do it in a way that is meaningful and valuable to the whole. Complexity science is required to work out how to do that, combined with leadership that sets the ethos, credos, sagacity and purpose of the organisation.

We understand that the long-term sustainability of any enterprise or organisation, or ecological niche, is dependent on its ability to be sufficiently diverse and sufficiently efficient – to stay within the window of viability. Too much diversity or too much efficiency is a risk to survival. The cognitive function of an organisation is the mechanism by which it makes sense of whether it is within a window of viability, or whether it is at risk of going down one extreme or the other.

The reason organisations veer out of the window of viability is not always lack of information. Lack of awareness, poor decision-making and lack of accurate contextualisation of that information can also be points of failure – again, with Kodak as an example of a company that overlooked the *creative destruction* of digital technology.

To stay within the window of viability, especially when the environment is changing on a continually accelerating basis, requires increasing ability – at the individual and the organisation level – to perform cognitive processes accurately and effectively. If we look at our staff and the technologies that support them through the lens of being a cognitive agent, this changes the view of what that individual needs in order to do their job: what degrees of freedom they need, and how our organisational policies and design may have restricted them until now. If we restrict our people – who are the best sensors to understand how the environment is changing – that reduces their effectiveness.

Building from the individual level of cognition, there is also a collective cognition for the organisation as a whole. We need to be sure we understand enough about our environment to know we are on the right trajectory. The right trajectory here is the one that keeps us within the window of viability, and at the same time maximising what is possible to achieve.

The window of viability is different for every organisation and every individual. Part of being a cognitively astute organisation is to invest time and effort understanding the window of viability, based on the organisation's purpose, goals and values. For an organisation that is operating in several different ecosystems, how can it stay viable in them all? To answer this question, we need to understand the important causal flows or causal processes that are essential to that ecosystem, and to ensure we are well-positioned within that causal network.

The reason we need to explicitly recognise the need to develop cognitive capabilities as an organisation is because understanding our positioning in our ecosystem and how that is changing on an instant basis, from one second to another, is essential to becoming and remaining a successful enterprise in the emerging technological era.

## Early Warning of Changes in the Operating Environment Using Information Theory

One of the more useful tools in the complexity scientist's toolbox is information theory. Now, don't worry, I'm not going to dive into this much, but I do want to talk about the central concept to information theory: Shannon entropy (also known as information entropy).

In 1952, Claude Shannon – a research engineer at Bell Laboratories – was tasked to invent a method for improving the transmission of information between a transmitter and a receiver. His invention – which he called 'a mathematical theory of communication' – was based on a very simple idea: surprising events carry more information than routine events. In other words, if you wake up in the morning and the sun has turned green, then that is going to jolt you into a hyper-aware state of mind, where your brain is working overtime to try and make sense of what is going on. When our interactions with friends or our environment reveal information that we were not expecting, we seek to make sense of it. We process that information more consciously.

This response to surprise is no different whether we are individuals (a friend's view on a film), in a team (discovering that a colleague is also a part-time taxidermist), an organisation (the sacking of a well-respected CEO) or an entire country (the death of Princess Diana). We seek to understand the causes of the surprising information, and as we do so we traverse Judea Pearl's Ladder of Causation. However, there is one key difference. When we are dealing with a complex system, or situation, there is uncertainty over cause-and-effect. This uncertainty is the result of a structural motif of a complex system – feedback loops – that leads to non-linear behaviour (as described in Chapter 5).

This level of surprise, as information, is measured in binary digits (bits). The more unlikely an event is, the higher the information generated by its occurrence. Let me illustrate this with the example of flipping a coin.

When you flip an unbiased coin there is a 50/50 chance of its landing on heads or tails. Both events are equally probable and so our uncertainty about the outcome is at a maximum. We cannot have more certainty that the coin will land heads up. Here, the Shannon Entropy of flipping an unbiased coin is 1 bit, which is the maximum information that can be obtained from a system (a coin flip) that can only generate two outcomes (heads or tails).

Now, let's assume that we've been given a biased coin that always lands on tails. We know that the coin is biased and so there is no surprise for us when the coin always lands on tails. If there is no surprise, then there is no information. The chance of the coin landing on tails is 100%. In this case, the Shannon entropy is 0 bits. Certainty does not yield new information.

We don't need to be too concerned with whether something is 1 bit, or 0.5

bit, or 0 bits or whatever. The point I am making here is that the greater the uncertainty we have about something, the greater the information we can gain from that situation. Likewise, if we have total certainty then there is no information, no knowledge, to be gained. Intuitively this makes sense – if I am observing something that is not changing then I am not learning anything new about it.

However, if I perturb that system – add a component, remove a component – then I may be cajoling the system into a different state. This new state may yield new information, especially if I have managed to move the system into an improbable state. (Incidentally, this is why the modes of creativity discussed in Chapter 4 – breaking, bending, blending – are fundamental to discovering new knowledge.)

For Shannon entropy to be used in more practical ways, a probabilistic model of a system would need to be constructed. This simply means that we have identified the different states that a system can occupy, and we have estimated the likelihood of the system being in that state at a moment in time. We can construct a probabilistic model through observing and recording the frequency with which different states are observed. If we observe the system in a given state more frequently over time, we may infer that the system is more likely to be found in that state at a future point. We need to capture enough of the history of the system to have sufficient confidence in the probabilistic model we are building. This learning takes time and requires continual sampling of the environment; and there are some challenges to solve – like how to represent the environment – but the idea is to invest time in building a probability distribution, a probabilistic model, of our environment. Novelty represents a previously unseen state and so that too should trigger a response, not least requiring an update of our probabilistic model.

As we build our probabilistic model, we are forming a hypothesis, an untested belief, about how the environment behaves. Every time we observe and capture the state of the system, we are testing that hypothesis. The Law of Large Numbers is relevant here. We expect to see a system move in and out of different states. It may spend more time in one state than we have observed before, or the opposite. We would need to see a persistent, recurring change in the frequency with which each state of the system is observed before we begin to suspect that our hypothesis of the system may need to be re-visited.

Now that we have constructed a probabilistic model of our environment (or, indeed, any system of interest), we can calculate its Shannon Entropy. If we have a good degree of confidence that our probabilistic model is sufficiently correct, then we can baseline these measures. We can then set a sampling rate of how often we re-calculate the Shannon Entropy of the probabilistic model (we may use machine learning techniques to optimise the sampling rate). If the Shannon Entropy measurement begins to diverge from the baseline value – by some pre-determined tolerance – then we could infer that the system may be changing in some way. This out-of-tolerance measurement could flag the need for further investigation either by an intelligent agent or a human.

What I am describing here is an idea. I am not aware of any existing technique, or concept, that achieves this. Neither do I know if there is much utility in what I have described. I believe it is technically feasible – the computational complexity of updating a probabilistic model and calculating its Shannon entropy can be achieved in polynomial time (that is very efficiently). As such, you should interpret this for what it is: an idea that I hope interests' people enough to pursue it further.

I believe the utility of this technique – of parsing the environment and comparing it against a probabilistic model – could be an efficient way to manage a vast amount of automated monitoring of an environment for changes that may warrant further investigation. Of course, this 'further investigation' would call into play more expensive resources, such as AI and/or humans.

My motivation for conceiving this idea comes back to the need for any organisation to become highly proficient at anticipating change. If an environment changes in unexpected ways, then we want to be observing the change in real-time, rather than analysing after the event. Why is this important? If we are observing the genesis of an enduring change in our operating environment, then we can gain insights into the causes that led to that change.

Applying Shannon Entropy as an early warning system can signal an alarm that our knowledge of our environment may no longer be accurate. We can respond to these warning signals by expending effort to understand the changes that may be occurring. From this we may create new knowledge and update our semantic graph to represent that new understanding. The semantic graph is critical, because all our collective intelligence draws on it to make good decisions. If that semantic graph is erroneous or significantly out of date, the quality of our decisions is impacted. As an organisation harnesses AI to the fullest – where we are talking about millions, if not billions, of decisions being taken every second – an accurate semantic graph becomes a strategically important asset.

Anticipation gives us time to prepare; yet to accurately anticipate our environment we need to be open to detecting changes that suggest our understanding of the environment may no longer be sufficiently accurate.

I'd like to finish this discussion on information theory by making one final point. The use of information theory to measure the behaviour of a dynamic system is not a new concept. Indeed, information theory is one of the most promising tools in the complexity scientist's toolbox for unravelling the mysteries of a complex system.

One of the biggest challenges for the complexity scientist is gaining access to information about the system of interest. Most of the time we simply cannot access a complex system with the tools we have. To give just a few examples: the brain, the weather, genetics. It is neither practical, nor feasible, for a complexity scientist to have access to every element or aspect of systems of this kind. Yet we are not without hope.

If we can capture the signals, the data, the transmissions, from these systems then we can begin to understand the system, even though it is hidden from us. Of course, as we gain more knowledge of these systems, we can then devise precise interventions that may yield crucial insights that either confirm our hypotheses or take us completely by surprise.

Until recently, I had been researching the use of information theory to infer the causal architecture of a system. Techniques such as Feldman & Crutchfield's causal state reconstruction, Schreiber's Transfer Entropy, or Tononi's Integrated Information Theory were all part of my toolkit.

They are all valuable and can tell us something interesting about a complex system. However, they do not have the explanatory power of causality, as proposed by Judea Pearl, which is where my own research continues. I pass on this observation to those readers who may be more familiar with these subjects.

**A High-Level Schema of a Cognitive Enterprise**

Inspired by the human brain as an autopoietic system – where we seek to maintain our sense of self, and that sense of self separates us from others – I conceive of the cognitive enterprise in a similar way. Consider the four zones as depicted in Figure 19. This schema is analogous to a living cell with a membrane (the outer ring) in direct contact with the environment (note the perforated edge) with the remaining zones buffered somewhat from that environment.

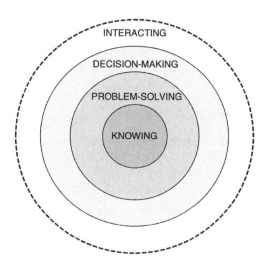

*Figure 19. A high-level map of the cognitive activities undertaken by humans and AI, individually or collectively, with the synthetic core as the central, unified and universal repository of all the collective knowledge of the organisation.*

The innermost zone I refer to somewhat mystically as Knowing. What I mean is that we operate from knowing what we know, and that the cognitive enterprise is geared to continually learn to expand our knowledge (as per the equation $KK > KU + UK + UU$ that I described in Chapter 6). This is an accurate model of the cognitive enterprise's operating environment as realised in the form of a synthetic core.

Next is the Problem-Solving zone, where the knowledge encoded in the synthetic core is used to make sense of the current situation and where a cognitive agent is equipped with tools to aid creativity and exploration.

The third zone are the specific functions required for Decision-Making: how we make evaluate a situation, explore options, forecast possible outcomes, determine what data or information we may need, and decide how to act, and so on.

Finally, on the outer ring, we have the zone I simply call Interacting. These are those activities that interact directly with an environment (internal, external or synthetic) to either detect changes in that environment, capture data and signals from that environment, and so on; or to actuate a decision and generate an effect within that environment.

The seamless interplay between these three different types of environment - synthetic, internal and external – is important to the cognitive enterprise. Each environment will be more useful for certain types of work, e.g., if we have AI doing hypothesis testing, it probably makes sense to do that in a synthetic environment. Then that might produce a recommendation for action in the real environment; or for more sensitive and high-risk activities, it might be developed further within the safer confines of the organisation.

Indeed, there could possibly be a progression of environments within which action takes place in the cognitive enterprise: synthetic → internal → external. We may seek to always experiment in the synthetic space first, because that is cheaper and faster and we can bring real-world, empirical data and knowledge into that space to validate our reasoning; then promising candidates for action are tested internally (if appropriate) so we can cast a more critical eye on them, and retain a degree of control over mitigating any unintended negative consequences; and then the best performers, the actions we think are going to have an impact that we desire, are deployed into the external environment. This is not a universal truth. The efficacy of an action may be dependent on a rapid and immediate effect in an external environment. And, of course, the rate of throughput through those environments will need to be sufficiently fast not to hinder action.

That synthetic – internal – external sequence happens already in most organisations; but use of synthetic environments – performing simulations and using computational models – tends to be low, except for engineering or tech-driven organisations. Most of what we currently see relating to innovation – testing prototypes or ideas – is within the internal environment, or with external focus groups.

In considering a world where most of our activities are online, it makes more sense to focus on the synthetic environment for broad testing of a wider range of options. That is a very different mindset.

For the engineer looking to build a cognitive enterprise, this high-level schema may provide a simple but different perspective from which to design and develop an enterprise architecture.

## How Might a Cognitive Enterprise Be Perceived?

One way to understand the difference between a cognitive enterprise and a traditional one is to think about the difference in the way it is experienced by various groups.

### *The Customer's View*

From a customer/user point of view, the response will be, 'They just always seem to know what I want. It just works. I don't really have to think about it. It's great.' A cognitive enterprise is in tune with what the people it serves are thinking at that time. This is why augmented reality is so exciting for the field of marketing.

For example, Apple is developing *Apple Glass* – a pair of glasses with a LIDAR sensor built into it which can do extremely accurate placement of virtual objects in our vision, as we are looking through a transparent display – and other companies have similar products.

As we walk through a shopping mall or drive down the road, a song might come on the radio, or the cameras on our autonomous car pick up something in the environment, and because of this uber-knowledge of next generation ad tech that understands our desires and preferences, we get pushed adverts or suggestions about what we might want to do. '200 yards here on the right is a really good steak house, with a 4.4 star rating on Trip Advisor.' That is the world we are moving into – getting into the heads of our customers.

To be effective at this involves tapping into belief systems also, which requires having a lot of information about our customers. This is another reason it is important to be a sagacious organisation, because with that power and deep insight into the behaviour and experience of a single individual human, come responsibility and accountability.

Organisations will have to uphold their trustworthiness and deliver according to a set of human-centric values and drivers for how they behave. Large companies are already starting to go down this route. Most of what Apple CEO Tim Cook talks about – whether at the developer conferences or in global announcements – relates to security and trust. Intel talks about trust. These big tech companies have realised that trust is almost sacred and is becoming a very important asset for an organisation.

This world is coming. The beginnings of it are evident now, and in ten years' time it will be close to fully evolved. Therefore, the cognitive enterprise needs to be responsive and adaptive and in tune with what is happening in the world, what resonates, and able, in addition, to uphold human-centric values.

## The Competitor's View

From the competitor's viewpoint, the actions of a cognitive enterprise look weird, and random. They ask, 'What are they doing? Why are they making that investment? That is just insane.' As discussed earlier, China is a prime example of this, investing billions into infrastructure projects and communications networks all around the world; and doing it at cost if not at a loss. In the traditional view, it doesn't make any sense, but in a cognitive advantage world, it is extremely smart.

It won't be until after an organisation has shifted the environment beyond recognition that the competitors will begin to understand what is happening.

This refers to the definition of cognitive advantage, to shape the environment at a pace that adversaries simply cannot continue to keep up, or even comprehend.

The second thing that would appear in a competitor's view of a cognitive enterprise is that it would appear busy. China appears busy and productive. What is happening, and the real reason they are doing these things, are obscured, not because they are being kept secret, but because of the scale, the apparent randomness, so that it is hard to keep up, and to pin down what they are doing. Once you've noticed one thing, they have invested in something else elsewhere.

Sun Tzu in the Art of War says one of the most powerful weapons is confusion – to confuse your enemy. For a cognitive enterprise pursuing a cognitive advantage trajectory, that is one of the benefits: to confuse the enemy. It can absorb a lot of an adversary's cognitive capacity just trying to keep track.

## *The Partner's View*

From the viewpoint of a partner organisation, a cognitive enterprise is loyal, trusted, has a clear vision and is good at communicating it to its partners. They know what they are doing and have a track record of achieving their aims. Everything they touch is gold. It isn't necessarily always perfect, but the over-riding experience is the sense of clarity.

Also, because a cognitive enterprise organisation excels at understanding its environment, predicting and anticipating and making active moves to shape that environment, those organisations tend to know more about their partners, and how they are performing in that environment, than even the partners know themselves. They can hold up a mirror and point out to trusted partners where they have blind spots. They might have a competitor on the horizon they are not paying enough attention to. The cognitive enterprise wants to look after its partners because it is dependent on them; it understands its dependencies in the ecosystem and invests in looking after those dependencies, which has enormous value to the partner. This is the true sense of the word partnership.

There is a need for precision in that partner relationship. The requirements a cognitive enterprise has of a partner are very precise. They know exactly what to ask. Sometimes that might be obscure, because the partner might not necessarily understand the bigger picture, the strategic foresight, and it is therefore important to be clear. A cognitive enterprise will educate its partners as well, where necessary.

Another perception that partners may have of a cognitive enterprise is the mastery of technology – specifically the technology that is relevant to each partner. A cognitive enterprise is precise in the tech and research investments it makes, embracing technological opportunities in a deliberate way.

Google is a good example of this. They have an almost overwhelming number of projects going on all the time. Everyone knows they are deliberate, bounded experiments and we admire them for that. Google Glass ran for a couple of years, then they scrapped it, saying they had learnt enough about it and now needed to go back, digest. They didn't try to cling on. They were in control of the trajectory of that technology, very deliberate and precise with the purpose of that project; and because they were precise and knew what they wanted from it, they could close it down with confidence.

## *Your Own People's View*

From the perspective of people who work within a cognitive enterprise, they love it, because in the same way the organisation excels at giving customers what they want, before they even know they need it, it applies that same power of insight to giving the best to its people. The way to get the best from people is to make them happy. Cognitive enterprises treat their people the same way they seek to develop a deep empathy for their customers.

# Chapter 9
# Building a Cognitive Advantage

*'The path isn't a straight line; it's a spiral. You continually come back to things you thought you understood and see deeper truths'*[37]

Barry H. Gillespie

## Goal 1. Develop Sagacious Leaders

One of the early challenges to building a cognitive advantage is to have a leadership team that is willing to invest their own time, and that of their organisation, in making profound changes to their culture.

Moving away from evaluating performance by one measure – total shareholder return – to the triple measures of profit, people and planet will be a considerable challenge. However, with climate change now requiring tangible and statutory action, and the power of social networks and the internet enabling citizen action in cyberspace to unmask that which was previously hidden by governments and companies, leadership teams now have to think and act with much greater awareness and ingenuity to balance these sometimes-competing demands.

Developing sagacious leaders – foresighted and wise, willing to be proven wrong and then do something about it – could well be the starting point in cultivating a long-term, sustainable change deep into the DNA of the organisation itself. But where to start? How *do* we develop sagacious leaders?

Elliot Jaques' work on complex information processing, and how different people have different levels of ability when it comes to processing complex information, could be a useful tool. He defined complex as rapidly changing information with large degrees of uncertainty.

His measure is about people's ability to embrace that uncertainty rather than be paralysed by it. I believe sagacious leaders reside at level 4 and 5, because these individuals tend to be creative in how they view problems and come up with solutions. As I explained in Chapter 6, the types of work that suit these types of thinkers are those that require re-defining and re-inventing what is most meaningful to their organisation.

Sagacious leaders do not have to be on the top team; but they do need the means to reach and influence people with their deep insights.

## Goal 2. Master Deep Insight to Complex Adaptive Systems

Data is now the raw material that your organisation is shaping into a valuable commodity. Data is no longer something that only the IT department needs care about. It is the precious resource at the heart of your new revenue streams and business models. You are going to have to reinvent your organisation to be data driven.

An investment is required to buy or generate data, analyse it, and use it to explore possible courses of action. This is digital transformation. The world has changed, there are now unfathomable amounts of data; we need to make sure we are providing our customers with the best experience, otherwise our competitors will; data can provide that insight.

It is important to understand the data that is valuable to your organisation. Data is your aperture into your own organisation and to your environment. However, data, like oil, requires effort to turn it into something valuable. So, where do you invest your effort? Do you invest in products and services that allows you to capture proprietary data? Or do you buy data from an ad tech firm, Facebook or a commercial data analysis company? Whatever it is, you need to have a data strategy.

There are many strategies and tactics that companies and governments can use to get to the data they want; but you need to understand what data you need in the first place. And you need to ensure that you have the correct legal and ethical practices in place to manage that data through its whole lifecycle.

This can be perceived as a chicken and egg problem, so it's worth starting small. The challenge here is that unless you can go out and buy a data analysis company, with data scientists and access to interesting proprietary data sets that are relevant to your organisation, you either need to outsource your data capabilities to a company that specialises in it, or you must grow your own, or develop it in partnership with another organisation.

To understand the data that is most important to you, you must go a little bit down the road towards developing capabilities in analysing and interpreting data. There is a feedback loop in understanding how your organisation needs to consume data to inform decisions: as you evaluate the results, that then allows you to be more selective about the kind of data you need to go after. It is a continuous cycle assisted by DevOps and Agile methodologies and enabled by commodotised cloud computing services such as IaaS (Infrastructure as a Service) and SaaS (Software as a Service) all with the aim of reducing the time-to-market of improvements to products and services.

Learning to manage this sea of data is important because it gets you on the route to being a data-savvy, data-driven organisation. That's the first challenge, to get on that trajectory. Then that sets you up for what comes next, where you begin to maximise your use of machine learning and specific techniques such as automated learning, and automated collection of data, including automated changes to where you source your data from. An optimisation process needs to happen. You will start to understand the relationship between data and automation. You are now ready to start taking the next step from data-driven to decision-centric.

As you become more data savvy you will start to create new business models, new products and new services. You may even be on your way to disrupting the industry your organisation has traditionally been a part of, because you are changing the rules of the game and making better decisions enabled by deeper, more profound insights to what your customers *really* want. To quote Jeff Bezos, 'If we can keep our competitors focused on us while we stay focused on the customer, ultimately we'll turn out all right'[38]. The data you use to inform yourself about how the environment is changing isn't the basis for beating your adversaries – you do so by changing the rules of the game.

## Goal 3. Develop the Agency to Act in Your Environment

As you become more data-driven, your organisation will be learning about how to behave in a different way – and how to compete differently. Changes may start to emerge; you are using data to continually improve your customer offering or your deals with partners, and this is shaping the environment to create the conditions for a mutually beneficial and sustainable, long-term relationship with your customers (consider for a moment Apple's success and how that is dependent on locking in customers to the value of their ecosystem).

Organisations succeed here because they have privileged access to data that yields insights that competitors simply do not have. This cultivates foresight and a strategic, long-term view. It is about dominating and mastering the environment you are operating in, which is a very different thing than just knowing how to turn data into product improvements. Agile, data-driven organisations may be very effective at responding to their environment, but only sagacious organisations are truly effective at shaping that environment.

When we're talking about transitioning an organisation from where it is now to being a cognitive enterprise, we need to take the critical members of the ecosystem on that journey with us. So, how do we influence the key members of our ecosystem – customers, partners, competitors, financiers – to operate in a way that supports our aims? Even better, how do we do that where mutual aims can be pursued? We need to set and explore the operational limits of our enterprise.

It may help to think about the organisation as an autopoietic system that is striving to sustain itself within a window of viability. In remaining viable, there will be dependencies – known and unknown – that extend beyond an organisation's direct control.

Understanding the operational limits of the organisation reflects the fact that there are many things in our environment that we as an organisation are critically dependent on; so, it makes sense to actively manage those dependencies. We need to think of how to position the organisation in the ecosystem to exert direct and indirect control of those critical dependencies most efficiently and effectively.

As a reminder, we are seeking to embrace data, disrupt or cultivate the ecosystems we currently operate in, and get into new ecosystems. We shouldn't rely on established ways of defining different industrial sectors – this can constrain how we frame the operational limits of our organisations.

These goals will take time to develop and implement, and how things will end up will not be clear at the start. We need to embrace uncertainty, to accept that we don't really know how this will pan out; in fact, part of the challenge is we don't understand enough about it, so we need to experiment and learn, to get a better understanding.

The lean start-up methodology will help us here: start small and scale up when we have confidence. We don't need to reinvent the methodologies and strategies for how we become a learning organisation. The idea of testing hypotheses for experimentation, which a Lean Start-up is built around, is the beginning of changing the culture to think about experimentation, and this is exactly what the cognitive enterprise is about: asking questions and improving our understanding of the environment through lots of experiments.

Where Eric Ries (the creator of the Lean Startup movement) talks about humans doing experiments, in a cognitive enterprise most of those experiments will be done by AI.

## Goal 4. Design and Deploy an Enterprise Architecture That Is Decision-Centric

A strategic enabler for taking an organisation from being data-driven, but still run primarily by humans, to a true collective intelligence, is to build the synthetic core of the organisation. The synthetic core codifies all the knowledge and understanding that human and artificial intellects have and share about the operating environment of the organisation.

If we accept that the transition to a cognitive enterprise is about maximising automation of decisions, then the synthetic core is the main enabler for that scale of automation. Your AI uses the synthetic core to inform its decisions.

This needn't take years to do. There is a bit of trial and error and prototyping. You can be intelligent about it and play around with a subset of the synthetic core that is particular to a market segment or to a specific product or service. Start by transitioning decisions in that one area from humans to AI. You will be building a *proto* version of the synthetic core as you do so.

There are many ways to break this down into tractable, achievable, and affordable steps. But do it quickly. Don't try to master this. You may be able to buy key components of the synthetic core – such as a semantic graph – from another organisation. Natural language processing models are a perfect example of a semantic graph you can buy, rather than developing from scratch yourself. Be smart. Use others. Ask your partners if they have been developing any relevant models.

Building a semantic graph is a tractable problem, but you must make a concerted effort to do it. Just as important is building the products and tools for humans and AI to access and leverage the value of the synthetic core.

Once we are on the way to building our cognitive enterprise, we can start measuring cognitive performance indicators. As we operate in our ecosystems, run our platforms, master the use of data to inform decisions, and do so on a reducing cycle time, and so on, performance indicators can tell us how quickly we are making decisions, and how quickly we are gaining insight into changes in our customers' and competitors' habits.

Fortunately, because we have invested in a profoundly capable machine that generates deep insights, we can apply that same powerful tool to understand ourselves, and whether we are maintaining ourselves in the window of viability.

## Goal 5. Maximise De-Centralisation of Authority and Accountability to Autonomous Cognitive Agents (Human and Artificial)

There is a simple logic to building the right culture for success: if we want to understand how the environment is changing, and adapt appropriately in the right timeframe, we need to allow cognitive agents who are closest to the environment and who directly interface into the environment, to influence the organisation's response. We need to equip cognitive agents with the means to make sense of how the environment is changing and empower them to make the changes they need to make to keep themselves relevant and viable in the pursuit of their goals.

This is one of the main motivations for autonomous, decentralised teams: empower people because they are the organisation's sensors into that domain of the environment; they have the domain wisdom, and they know the best way to react. Of course, decentralising does not guarantee success.

There is plenty of empirical evidence about the value of small teams, but we also must address the possibility of not having the right mix of minds in those teams. We run the risk of *group-think* where there is insufficient diversity of opinion and therefore things get missed, and bad decisions are made. Even with autonomous, decentralised teams you need to perturb them from time to time. Amazon do this by sacking ten percent of their workforce every year – arguably an inhumane approach to keeping everyone on their toes, as there are other ways to create grit in the machine.

There is an optimum point of autonomy, however, and rather than just think of these as teams of people, we need to think about them as autopoietic systems. As an autopoietic system, a small team of 6-8 people has an identity. These teams have a structural coupling with their environment; they have a semi-permeable boundary where they can bring in enough information about the environment that is useful and valuable, to signal whether they need to do something different. But also, enough freedom to determine the meaning of new information and, therefore, how they should act thus reinforcing their sense of identity and autonomy to act.

With autonomy comes responsibility and accountability which means these teams are responsible for their own performance, for understanding their needs and for securing the support they need from other teams with which to achieve their purpose efficiently and effectively.

You can start doing that in your organisation today. You don't need AI to do it. You can adopt the view of your organisation as a living entity, so the organisation is then a network of hierarchical, interconnected and cooperating autopoietic units.

A business is an autopoietic unit, a team is an autopoietic unit, an individual is an autopoietic unit. That's why I talk about the unit of analysis of the cognitive enterprise being the cognitive agent: it is synonymous with an autopoietic unit. Cognitive agent is a more compelling phrase because it includes our consideration of AI as also being an autopoietic unit.

There is a similarity here to the team of teams concept developed by General Stanley McChrystal. During the early 21$^{st}$ century War on Terror military campaigns in Afghanistan and Iraq, he observed that his forces needed to look and act like the small, self-contained, highly autonomous terrorist cells that they were fighting. This was a necessity if his forces were to keep pace with their enemy and to adapt quickly and often enough to prevail and to succeed. His concept was to create teams, each having a specific mission to accomplish, and with a high degree of awareness of their dependency on other teams. Teams had adjacent and interdependent objectives that promoted sharing of knowledge and insights. In my language, McChrystal's team of teams is a network of autopoietic units (both human and artificial) that are continually sensing, understanding and acting within their environment.

The keys to culture are responsibility and freedom both in the individual and in the collective sense. Allowing individuals and teams autonomy to take appropriate action as they see fit and providing support to ensure they can be accountable for those actions, will be essential.

All the good things that leaders and HR theorists aspire to – happy, productive people – are completely aligned with building a successful cognitive enterprise.

## Goal 6. Build a Culture that Deeply Values Sagacity

I believe that wisdom as we know it – deep sagacious insight – will be difficult for AI to replicate in the next 15-20 years. Unless we truly get to a general artificial intelligence, wisdom is probably the last bastion where humans add value in a cognitive sense. That's good – let's embrace that. We have freedom now to be creative and be compassionate.

One of our biggest problems is that people are stretched and stressed – whether through lack of money or lack of time or thinking your life is terrible because you've spent the last four hours on social media and everyone else's lives seem to be awesome. As we become less stressed, we become wiser, more insightful and more mindful, which in turn leads to being more compassionate to one another.

The cognitive enterprise, and pursuing a cognitive advantage trajectory, is not just about beating the competition. It has the potential to elevate humans to move onto the next stage of development of our civilisation. It could help to transform us in amazing ways. Machines give us more time and space to be human.

The need for more sagacious thinking has implications for recruitment and training – assessing the type of people who are going to succeed in a cognitive enterprise. This takes us back to Jaques' work on complex information processing. There will be a supervisory element to what humans do, and I think most people in work will be supervising machines rather than doing tasks themselves. Then we can spend most of our time operating at Jaques' higher levels of work (levels 4 - 7) where being creative, foresighted, sagacious, deeply insightful are commonplace. Jaques' complex information processing should be a helpful tool to think about the type of human workforce an organisation needs in order to pursue a cognitive advantage trajectory.

## The Future with Cognitive Advantage

Becoming a cognitive enterprise is about culture. In nature, we talk about competition and co-operation, even down to the biological level. An individual biological cell you could say is competing against other biological cells for resources – nutrients – from the environment. But at some point in our evolution multi-cellularity emerged as a viable form of organisation. Biological cells gave up direct competition with their neighbours, and different types of proteins evolved that were far less resource intensive. Through co-operation in a multi-cellular sense, everyone could survive better, because they were able to persist with a much lower energy requirement.

In conversation with a colleague about this book, he offered this insight: there is a tactical aspect to cognitive advantage and there is a holistic element to it. The tactical aspect is the ability to act at such a pace to shape your environment such that you compromise your adversaries' ability to comprehend and act in that environment. That is adversarial, a win/lose scenario; and nature has taught us the importance of cooperation and cultivation. There is a duality to cognitive advantage. One side is about winning, one is about cultivating.

Perhaps we need to embrace and accept that duality, that there are two aspects to what cognitive advantage can mean. At times you might have to be more competitive – because you know with your foresight that that is important for your long-term viability; but there is also the issue of trust – with customers and partners, and with the wider environment.

What we may gain from cognitive advantage, ultimately, is long-term viability of our communities, our organisations and even our civilisation.

Cognitive advantage enables us to recognise what is going on around us, and to deal with life, whatever happens; and it gives us a deeper insight to the impact of our own actions.

How we use that insight will shape our future civilisation.

# COGNITIVE ADVANTAGE

# References

**Chapter 1**

1    From Ray Kurzweil's *The Singularity is Near: When Humans Transcend Biology*, New York, Penguin, 2005.

2    From Nicky Case's *How To Become A Centaur*, Journal of Design and Science, DOI: 10.21428/61b2215c, 2018.

3    Definition of sagacity as described in the Cambridge Dictionary, University of Cambridge.

4    The origin of the phrase 'data is the new oil' is most often attributed to Clive Humby.

5    From Megan Friedl's news article 'Goldfein delivers Air Force update' published online at www.af.mil on September 19th 2017.

6    Samuel Taylor Coleridge, The Rime of the Ancient Mariner, first published in 1798.

7    From my own article that is due to be published as a chapter in Advances in Intelligent Systems and Computing, Vol. 1363, Springer Publishing, 2021.

**Chapter 2**

8    From Eddie Obeng's TED talk 'The World After Midnight' in June 2012.

9    Pachauri & Meyer's report: *Climate Change 2014: Synthesis Report, Contribution of Working Groups I, II and III to the Fifth Assessment*

*Report of the Intergovernmental Panel on Climate Change*. IPCC, Geneva, 2014.

10  Eliot Higgins in his recent book 'We Are Bellingcat' published by Bloomsbury, 2021.

11  As mentioned in the article 'Seven Technological Advancements That Make Singapore a Smart City' on the iotforall.com website.

12  Concluding remarks in the workshop 'Harnessing Complexity and Data Science to Develop Urban Solutions for Singapore'.

**Chapter 3**

13  Whilst widely attributed to Stephen Hawking there is, in fact, no evidence that he ever said this. The earliest record of this phrase being used was in 1903 in the journal *L'Annee Psychologique*. The exact phrase was '*la faculte de s'adapter*'.

14  Definition as retrieved from the Lexico dictionary website (www.lexico.com) run by the University of Oxford, UK.

15  From the seminal book 'The Realization of the Living' by Humberto Maturana and Francisco Varela and published by Springer in 1980.

16  Definition as retrieved from the Lexico dictionary website (www.lexico.com) run by the University of Oxford, UK.

17  From Jennifer Rowley's article in the Journal of Information Science titled 'The Wisdom Hierarchy: Representations of the DIKW hierarchy', published in 2007.

**Chapter 4**

18  From Alan Turing's seminal paper on artificial intelligence titled 'Computing Machinery and Intelligence' published in MIND in 1950.

19     Quote taken from David Poole, Alan Mackworth and Randy Goebel book 'Computational Intelligence' published in 1998 by Oxford University Press.

20     From Bergstein's interview with Judea Pearl in January 2020 and subsequently published in the article 'What AI still can't do' in MIT Technology Review.

21     From Twitter user Nikita Jerschow (@nikita_jerschow) on August 21st 2020.

22     From Sam Altman's tweet on July 19th 2020. His Twitter handle is @sama.

23     From the article 'Doctor GPT-3: hype or reality?' written by the research team at Nabla (www.nabla.com) who discovered the unnerving (and clearly unintentional) behaviour of GPT-3.

24     From Adam Santoro and co-authors blog post published on 11 July 2018 on deepmind.com.

25     From Elias Bareinboim's online tutorial video available from https://crl.causalai.net.

26     From Bill Schmarzo's article 'Design Thinking Humanizes Data Science' published on January 3rd 2019 on the datasciencecentral.com website.

**Chapter 5**

27     From Stephen Hawking's 'millenium' interview given on 23 January 2000.

28     From Carlo Rovelli's article 'Quantum weirdness isn't weird – if we accept objects don't exist' published in the New Scientist on March 10th 2021.

29    From a news briefing that Donald Rumsfeld gave on February 12<sup>th</sup> 2002 (archived on defense.gov website).

**Chapter 6**

30    From Ralph Stacey's book 'Complexity and Organisational Reality' published by Routledge in 2010.

**Chapter 7**

31    From David Adam's article 'What if aging weren't inevitable, but a curable disease?' published 19<sup>th</sup> August 2019 in MIT Technology Review.

32    From Gwern Branwen's comprehensive journal which can be found at gwern.net.

33    From an interview with Takehiko Kakikuchi as reported in Kana Inagaki and Leo Lewis's article 'Building an extensive intelligence network to know your markets' published on the Financial Times website (ft.com) on August 9<sup>th</sup> 2020.

34    From Marcus Aurelius 'Meditations' published by Penguin Classics.

**Chapter 8**

35    From Napoleon Bonaparte's book 'Napoleon: In His Own Words', Kessinger Publishing, 2010

36    From Stuart Kauffman's book 'Investigations' published by Oxford University Press in 2002

## Chapter 9

37   A wonderful quote from an article written by Barry H. Gillespie titled 'Truthfulness: Much More Than Not Telling Lies' which was published on the elephantjournal.com website on July 26th 2013.

38   From Tara-Nicholle Nelson's article 'Obsess Over Your Customers, Not Your Rivals' published on the Harvard Business Review website (hbr.org) on May 11th 2017.

# Bibliography

Ackoff, Russell, *From Data to Wisdom*, Journal of Applied Systems Analysis 16, pp. 3-9, 1989

Agrawal, Ajay, Gans, Joshua, Goldfarb, Avi, *Prediction Machines: The Simple Economics of Artificial Intelligence*, Boston, Harvard Business Review Press, 2018

Ascher, Jan, Tonies, Fleur, *How To Turn Everyday Stress Into 'Optimal Stress'*, McKinsey Quarterly, 18 Feb 2021, viewed: 4 Apr 2021

Ashby, Ross, *An Introduction to Cybernetics*, Martino Fino Books, 2015

Awalegaonkar, Ketan, et al., *AI: Built To Scale*, Accenture Research Report, 14 Nov 2019, viewed: 10 Apr 2021

Ballerini, et al., *Interaction ruling animal collective behaviour depends on topological rather than metric distance: Evidence from a field study*, PNAS, 105(4), pp.1232-1237, 2008

Bareinboim, Elias, et al., *On Pearl's Hierarchy and the Foundations of Causal Inference*, Columbia CausalAI Laboratory, Technical Report (R-60), 2020

Barrett, David, et al., *Measuring abstract reasoning in neural networks*, Proceedings of the 35th International Conference on Machine Learning,

Stockholm, Sweden, PMLR 80, 2018

Benaich, Nathan, Hogarth, Ian, *State of AI Report*, stateof.ai, 1 Oct 2020, viewed: 15 Dec 2020

Case, Nicky, *How To Become A Centaur*, Journal of Design and Science, DOI: 10.21428/61b2215c, 2018

Chessell, Mandy, *Ethics for Big Data and Analytics*, IBM Corporation, 2014

Conklin, Jeff, *Wicked Problems and Social Complexity*, Chapter 1 in Dialogue Mapping: Building Shared Understanding of Wicked Problems, Wiley, 2005

Cover, Thomas, Thomas, Joy, *Elements of Information Theory*, Wiley-Interscience, 2006

Creel, Herrlee, *Confucius and the Chinese Way*, New York, Harper, 1949

Dalio, Ray, *Principles: Life and Work*, Simon & Schuster, 2017

Doll, Richard, Hill, Austin, *Smoking and Carcinoma of the Lung*, British Medical Journal, 2(4682): pp. 739-748. 1950

Dorrier, Jason, *OpenAI's GPT-3 Algorithm Is Now Producing Billions of Words a Day*, singularityhub.com, 4 Apr 2021, viewed: 5 Apr 2021

Eagleman, David, Brandt, Anthony, *The Runaway Species: How Human*

*Creativity Remakes the World*, Catapult, 2017

Friedl, Megan, *Goldfein delivers Air Force update*, af.mil, 19 Sep 2017, viewed: 5 May 2020

Friston, Karl, *The free-energy principle: a unified brain theory?*, Nature Reviews Neuroscience, 11, 127-138, 2010

Gilchrist, Alasdair, *Industry 4.0: The Industrial Internet of Things*, Apress, 2016

Government Communications Headquarters, *Pioneering a New National Security: The Ethics of Artificial Intelligence*, Crown Publishing, 2021

Graham, Pauline, *Mary Parker Follett Prophet of Management*, Beard Books, 2003

Harvey, Phil, *Breaking Bard: Using Microsoft AI to unlock Shakespeare's greatest works*, news.microsoft.com, 23 Apr 2019, viewed: 30 Dec 2020

Jogalekar, Ashutosh, *Stephen Hawking's advice for twenty-first century grads: Embrace complexity*, scientificamerican.com, 23 April 2013, viewed: Sep 2020

Handy, Charles, *Understanding Organisations*, Penguin Publishing, 2015

Hemp, Paul, *Death by Information Overload*, Harvard Business Review, 2009

Higgins, Eliot, *We Are Bellingcat: An Intelligence Agency for the People*, Bloomsbury Publishing, 2021

Ho, Peter, *Complexity and Urban Governance*, Vienna, 2015

Jaques, Elliot, Cason, Kathryn, *Human Capability: A Study of Individual Potential and its Application*, Cason Hall & Co Publishers, 1994

Kasparov, Garry, *Deep Thinking: Where Machine Intelligence Ends and Human Creativity Begins*, London, John Murray, 2017

Kauffman, Stuart, *Investigations*, Oxford University Press, 2002

Klyubin, Alexander, et al., *Representations of Space and Time in the Maximization of Information Flow in the Perception-Action Loop*, Neural Computation 19, pp. 2387-2432, 2007

Kurzweil, Ray, *The Singularity is Near: When Humans Transcend Biology*, New York, Penguin, 2005

Lietaer, Bernard, et al., *Towards a Sustainable World: 3 Paradigm Shifts*, Vienna, Delta Institute, 2019

Leviathan, Yaniv, *Google Duplex: An AI System for Accomplishing Real-World Tasks Over the Phone*, ai.googleblog.com, 8 May 2018, viewed: 15 Oct 2020

Luhmann, Niklas, *Theory of Society Volume 1 and 2*, Stanford University

Press, 2013

Luisi, Pier Luigi, *Autopoiesis: a review and a reappraisal*, Naturwissenschaften, 90(20), pp. 49-59, 2003

Marcus, Gary, Davis, Ernest, *Rebooting AI: Building Artificial Intelligence We Can Trust*, Pantheon, 2019

Maslow, Abraham, *A Theory of Human Motivation*, Psychological Review, 50(4), pp. 370-396, 1943

Maturana, Humberto, Varela, Francisco, *Autopoiesis and Cognition: The Realization of the Living*, Springer, 1980

McChrystal, Stanley, *Team of Teams: New Rules of Engagement for a Complex World*, Penguin, 2015

McCulloch, Warren, Pitts, Walter, *A Logical Calculus of the Ideas Immanent in Nervous Activity*, Bulletin of Mathematical Biophysics, 5(4), pp. 115-133, 1943

Minsky, Marvin, Papert, Seymour, *Perceptrons: An Introduction to Computational Geometry*, 1969

Moore, Martin, *Democracy Hacked: Political Turmoil and Information Warfare in the Digital Age*, Oneworld Publications, 2018

Merton, Robert, *Social Theory and Social Structure*, New York, Free Press,

1949

Nassehi, Armin, *Organizations as decision machines: Niklas Luhmann's theory of organized social systems*, The Sociological Review, 2005

Norton, Steven, *Era of AI-Powered Cyberattacks Has Started*, wsj.com, 15 Nov 2017, viewed: 30 Apr 2020

Obeng, Eddie, *Smart Failure for a Fast-Changing World*, TEDGlobal2012, June 2012

Osinga, Frans, *Science, Strategy and War: The Strategic Theory of John Boyd (Strategy and History)*, Routledge, 2006

Pachauri, R.K. and Meyer, L.A. (eds), *Climate Change 2014: Synthesis Report, Contribution of Working Groups I, II and III to the Fifth Assessment Report of the Intergovernmental Panel on Climate Change*. IPCC, Geneva, 2014.

Panda, Jayshree, *The Weaponization of Artificial Intelligence*, forbes.com, 14 Jan 2019, viewed: 10 May 2020

Parker, Geoffrey, Van Alstyne, Marshall, Choudary, Sangeet, *Platform Revolution*, New York, W.W. Norton & Company, 2016

Pearl, Judea, Mackenzie, Dana, *The Book of Why: The New Science of Cause and Effect*, Allen Lane, 2018

BIBLIOGRAPHY

Poole, David, Mackworth, Alan, Goebel, Randy, *Computational Intelligence: A Logical Approach*, Oxford University Press, 1998

Porter, Jack, *Kasparov v Computer: When Deep Blue Beat The Grandmaster*, 1 May 2020, viewed: 10 May 2020

Reese, Eric, *The Lean Startup: How Constant Innovation Creates Radically Successful Businesses*, Portfolio Penguin, 2011

Reinsel, David, Gantz, John, Rydning, John, *The Digitization of the World: From Edge to Core*, IDC White Paper US44413318, 2018

Reynolds, Matt, *DeepMind's AI beats world's best Go player in latest face-off*, newscientist.com, 23 May 2017, viewed: 2 Apr 2020

Richards, Chet, *Certain to Win: The Strategy of John Boyd, Applied to Business*, Xlibris Corp, 2004

Richter, Felix, *Amazon Leads $130-Billion Cloud Market*, statista.com, 4 Feb 2021, viewed: 5 Apr 2021

Rittel, Horst, Webber, Melvin, *Dilemmas in a General Theory of Planning*, Policy Sciences, 4(2), pp. 155-169, 1973

Robbs, John, *Brave New War: The Next Stage of Terrorism and the End of Globalization*, John Wiley & Sons, 2007

Rovelli, Carlo, *Quantum weirdness isn't weird – if we accept objects don't exist*, newscientist.com, 10 Mar 2021, viewed: 20 Mar 2021

Rowley, Jennifer, *The Wisdom Hierarchy: Representations of the DIKW hierarchy*, Journal of Information Science, 33(2), pp. 163-180, 2007

Russell, Stuart, *Human Compatible: AI and the Problem of Control*, Allen Lane, 2019

Russell, Stuart, Norvig, Peter, *Artificial Intelligence: A Modern Approach*, 3rd edition, Pearson, 2016

Schumacher, Ernst, *Small Is Beautiful: A Study of Economics as if People Mattered*, Vintage, 1993

Shannon, Claude, *A Mathematical Theory of Communication*, The Bell System Technical Journal, Vol. 27, pp. 379-423, 1948

Silver, David, et al. *A general reinforcement learning algorithm that masters chess, shogi, and Go through self-play*, Science, DOI: 10.1126/science.aar6404, 2018

Spetzler, Carl, Winter, Hannah, Meyer, Jennifer, *Decision Quality: Value Creation from Better Business Decisions*, Wiley, 2016

Stacey, Ralph, *Complex Responsive Processes in Organizations: Learning and Knowledge Creation*, London, Routledge, 2001

Susskind, Daniel, *A World Without Work*, London, Allen Lane, 2020

Taleb, Nassim Nicholas, *The Black Swan: the impact of the highly improbable*, 2nd edition, London, Penguin, 2010

Thaler, Richard, Sunstein, Cass, *Nudge: Improving Decisions About Health, Wealth and Happiness*, Penguin, 2012

The Forum for Ethical AI, *Democratising decisions about technology: a toolkit*, Royal Society of Arts publication, 2019

Thomson, Amy, *Google Shows AI Can Spot Breast Cancer Better Than Doctors*, www.bloomberg.com, 2 Jan 2020, viewed: 5 May 2020

Turing, Alan, *Computing Machinery and Intelligence*, MIND A Quarterly Review, No. 236, 1950

Turner, Anthony, *Generation Z: Technology and Social Interest*, Journal of Individual Psychology. 71(2): 103-113, 2015

Tzu, Sun, *The Art of War*, Clearbridge Publishing, 2014

Ulanowicz, Robert, et al., *Quantifying sustainability: resilience, efficiency and the return of information theory*, Ecological Complexity, 6(1):27-36, 2009

Various authors of Statista Report, *Digital Economy Compass 2019*, Statista, 2019

Virgo, Nathaniel, et al., *The Role of the Spatial Boundary in Autopoiesis*,

Advances in Artificial Life – Darwin meets von Neumann – 10th European Conference, ECAL 2009, Budapest, Hungary, pp.13-16, 2009

Von Hippel, Eric, *Democratizing Innovation*, London, The MIT Press, 2005

Weizenbaum, Joseph, *ELIZA – A Computer Program for the Study of Natural Language Communication Between Man and Machine*, Communications of the ACM, 1966

Wiener, Norbert, *Cybernetics: Or Control and Communication in the Animal and the Machine*, Martino Fino Books, 2013

Wiseman, Liz, *Multipliers: How the Best Leaders Make Everyone Smart*, Harper Business, 2017

# BIBLIOGRAPHY

If you have enjoyed

Cognitive Advantage

then please do visit my blog at **richardjoncarter.com** where
I regularly post on topics related to cognitive advantage.